Happy Cooking + Merry Christmas
2013!

Love,

♥ Anne + Daniel

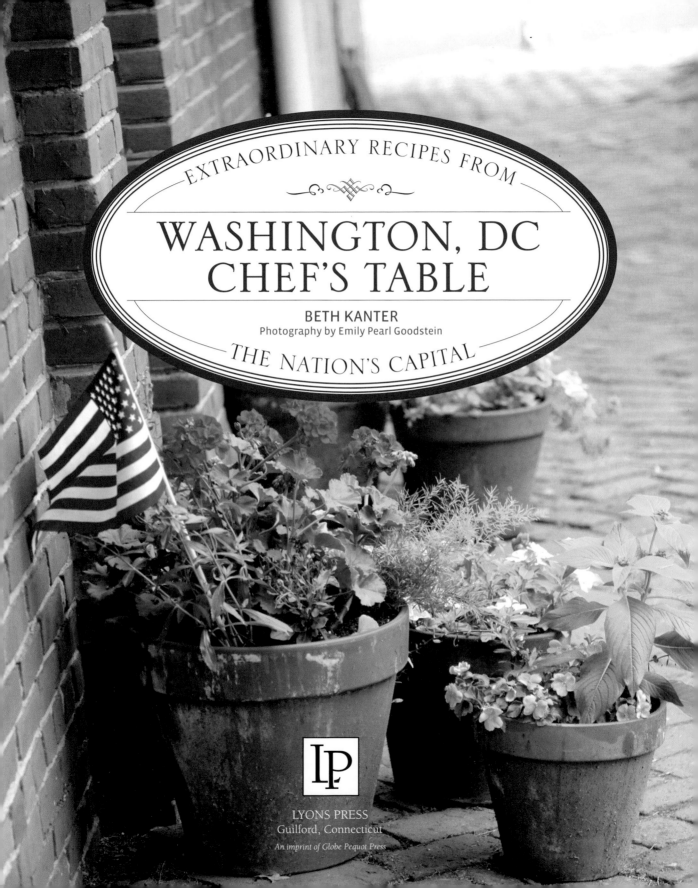

EXTRAORDINARY RECIPES FROM

WASHINGTON, DC CHEF'S TABLE

BETH KANTER

Photography by Emily Pearl Goodstein

THE NATION'S CAPITAL

LYONS PRESS
Guilford, Connecticut
An imprint of Globe Pequot Press

For Gabriel and Miriam for being delicious . . .

Editor: Amy Lyons
Project Editor: David Legere
Text Design: Libby Kingsbury
Layout Artist: Nancy Freeborn

Library of Congress Cataloging-in-Publication Data is available on file.

ISBN 978-0-7627-8148-5

Printed in the United States of America

10 9 8 7 6 5 4 3 2 1

Restaurants and chefs often come and go, and menus are ever-changing.
We recommend you call ahead to obtain current information before
visiting any of the establishments in this book.

More Praise for Washington, DC Chef's Table

"The incredible recipes from DC's top chefs are reason enough to own this book, but for food lovers, it's also an invaluable guide to the city's best places to eat, from food trucks to fine dining. The recipes include some of my all-time favorite restaurant dishes, which I'll now be recreating at home."

— Amanda McClements, food writer and owner of Salt & Sundry

"This cookbook reminds me on every page why I love DC's vibrant restaurant scene. Kanter has curated an all-star cast of the capital region's top chefs and their most winning dishes, which taste good no matter where you live."

— Nevin Martell, Food Writer (the *Washington Post, Plate*)

"The *Washington, DC Chef's Table* is a beautiful collection of divine, covetable recipes from some of the best chefs in DC but also in the country."

—Lynne Breaux, President of Restaurant Association Metropolitan Washington

"*Washington, DC Chef's Table* doesn't only find some of the city's best chefs—both traditional and cutting edge—but it tells you their story and lets you in on the secrets of some of their tastiest recipes. You can sample the city's best food—and then cook it yourself."

—Martin Andres Austermuhle, Editor-in-Chief, DCist.com

"The *Washington DC Chef's Table* does an excellent job of capturing the stories of some of DC's most well-known chefs. Beth Kanter artfully weaves in their memories and anecdotes into the recipes, giving the reader a better sense of the people behind the food. Washingtonians will be proud of our city's culinary talent and proud to have this cookbook on their bookshelves."

—Marissa Bialecki, Food writer and editor for WeLoveDC.com

Contents

Acknowledgments

Anyone who has ever peeked into a restaurant kitchen knows that it takes many hands to create a beautiful meal. The same holds true for writing a book, especially a book about food. There have been so many skilled and supportive hands along the way who have helped turn *Washington, DC Chef's Table* from idea to book. First and foremost among them are the talented chefs of this great town whose recipes, stories, and images grace the pages of book. Thank you for lending your time and talent to this project as well as for pulling back the curtain long enough for us see the magic of your craft.

An amazing group of professionals have helped with everything from arranging photo shoots to setting up chef interviews to signing releases. Along with the chefs, we could also not have done it without your helpful hands e-mailing, dialing, and troubleshooting along the way. Huge thank yous to Anthony Hesselius and the team at Linda Roth Associates; Jennifer Motruk Loy at JML marketing + communications; Jennifer Resick Williams of Know Public Relations; Sue-Jean Chun, Meaghan Donohoe, Cameron Feller, and the rest of simoneink, llc; Heather Freeman, Scott Homstead, and Lindley Thornburg and their team at Heather Freeman Media & Public Relations; Renee Sharrow and her colleagues at the Park Hyatt; Amber Pfau and Sangeetha Sarma at Pfau Communications; Stephanie Salvador and the rest of the team at ThinkFoodGroup; Shayla Martin; Stephanie Betteker; Kate Manecke; Jennie Kuperstein; Jacqueline Herrera; Rachel Hayden; Molly J. Stephey; Ashley Lawson and John Murphy at Miriam's Kitchen; Tricia Barba; Jordyn Lazar; Madeline Block; Atul Narain; Sean-Patrick Applegate; Tseday Gizaw; Sandra Holley; Neidra Holmstrom; Jennie Kuperstein; and Nina Kocher. Also a shout-out to Danielle Tergis and Laura Genello for allowing us to photograph at the always perfectly in season Dupont Circle FRESHFARM Market.

I am very grateful to Amy Lyons for once again giving me the opportunity to write about the city I love so. It's always a pleasure to work with you. Thank you to David Legere and everyone at Globe Pequot Press for all of your help with *Washington, DC Chef's Table* and for all you do to turn a computer file into a book.

I am beyond lucky to have so many people in my day-to-day life who have helped me along the way, including a wonderful circle of friends who despite their own busy lives always lent their hands for editing, recipe-testing, eating, pep-talking, crowd sourcing, and informal frog-leg-polling. Among them are the forever fabulous Alyson Weinberg, Lisa Kanter, Gayle Neufeld, Laurie Moskowitz, Soo Ji Min, Jackie Eyl, Jennifer Haber, and Melissa Hecht. Among the many gifts the wonderful Elissa Froman has brought into my life is introducing me to Emily Goodstein, the person responsible for all the incredible images in this book. Emily, it has been a pure delight to work with you. I am in awe of your talent and your outlook on life (both behind and away from the camera) to say nothing of your social media, spreadsheet, and Google Docs skills. Thank you for photographing this wild ride and thank you for your friendship.

I am not sure what I would do without Jeff Goodell in my life and I am very happy I don't have to find out. One thing I do know is that without him my desk would be taken over by used mugs and yesterday's dishes, and that I would laugh a whole lot less. Thank you for being you. Gabriel and Miriam, the other reasons for my smile, thank you for being your yummy selves. I have to take a moment of parental privilege and document that Miriam started reading the day before I finished this book and that Gabe learned how to make sushi midway through the manuscript. Everything else is just commentary.

—BK

It has been quite a journey between the phone call from Beth asking me to photograph this book to the moment when I broke the binding of *Washington, DC Chef's Table*. My fellow travelers have included divine friends, volunteer drivers, taste testers, camera bag holders, and cheerleaders.

To Amy Lyons at Globe Pequot Press, thanks for believing I was the right photographer for this project.

Thanks to Amber Wobschall and Jeremy Bratt for starting their hand-modeling careers at the other end of my camera lens.

Gratitude to Amanda Boone, Sally Heaven, Rachel Hillman, Sara Hoffman, Jackie Mathis, and Caroline Stuart, who left the comfort of their cubicles to be photographed while dining on food-truck delicacies.

A shout-out to my ideas man, Julie Finkelstein, who perfected the list of rules to follow when dining out with a food photographer.

Much appreciation to Molly Amster, Jodi Bart, Amy Born, Natalie Cole, Cara Fisher, Rebecca Goodstein, Beth Kurtz, Lance Melton, Sarah Rosenfeld, and Jill Stepak, who drooled over preview photos, donned bee suits, made sure I didn't fall off of various chairs while trying to get the perfect angle, and encouraged me to say yes to this life-changing opportunity.

Mom and Dad, I'm sorry I protested the *palak paneer* and bouillabaisse you fed me when I was little. It is because of you that I now have such an appreciation of good food and the people who make it.

And last, I am eternally grateful for the supreme connector that is Elissa Froman, who introduced me to my favorite collaborator, Beth Kanter. Beth, your genuine spirit and kind energy are an inspiration, and I am truly honored that we could share this delicious adventure together.

—EPG

Introduction

Sometime during the last handful of years it has become acceptable, almost in vogue, to refer to Washington, DC, as not "real America." I've noticed it of late in speeches, campaign ads, and punctuating cable network news banter. What I think they don't understand is that beyond the monuments and the marble, Washington, DC, is a hometown. An all-American hometown. A hometown with its own rhythm, its own buzz, and its own soul, all of it twisting, turning, and spinning together against the breathtaking backdrop of some of our country's most recognizable landmarks. And, like any other hometown beyond the Beltway, Washington, DC, is a place that is rich with stories. *Washington, DC Chef's Table* is about all these stories. While what you hold in your hands is most definitely a photo-rich cookbook filled with an incredible mix of recipes from the city's best restaurants, it also very much is a storybook. A volume of narratives told in cups of flour, cooking times, and mixing instructions. It is a book of family lore spoken through food and tales of relationships, friendships, and even a pie in the sky (or pasta, poached eggs, or pudding in the sky) dream or two communicated via grilling, marinating, or roasting guidelines. The stunning photos of the completed dishes in many ways are family photos.

What unifies the vast majority of the people behind the recipes—the stories—in this book is that they come from a deep-rooted tradition of feeding others. Chefs like Ris Lacoste, who cooks many of her mother's beloved dishes at her West End restaurant, or Marc Vidal of Boqueria, who as a boy spent his time before and after school at his mother's restaurant. Similarly, others you will meet on these pages take to their kitchens to whip up special-occasion dishes from their childhoods, like Danny Bortnick, who went against fine-dining conventional wisdom when he added his family's matzoh ball soup to the Firefly menu, or Dennis Marron of Poste Moderne Brasserie, whose smoked trout rillettes stand as an homage to a '60s-era butter-and-canned-fish hors d'oeuvre his mom made for company. In fact, the first draft of this book included a chapter of family recipes that chefs serve at their restaurants, like the Yum Beef Salad at Beau Thai that Aschara Vigsittaboot learned to make from her mother and the bouillabaisse Cathal Armstrong learned to compose from his father. But that chapter quickly was turning into a book of its very own, since strong family ties bind many a Washington, DC, kitchen. Many of the other recipes in this book are also elaborate taste tributes to places from the past that hold special meaning to chefs, like Kazuhiro "Kaz" Okochi's sea trout napoleon, Haidar Karoum's ramps at Estadio, or the avocado banana *chaat* Vikram Sunderam created for Rasika.

These recipes, along with so many others that make up *Washington, DC Chef's Table,* serve as personal histories of people, place, and time. And, taken together, each and every recipe, chef profile, and photo in this book tells a part of a bigger story—the story of how our city, our hometown, embraces and defines its identity a bit more with each passing day and year. Some go back decades and center on neighborhoods, families, and the good old-fashioned American know-how of people like Ben and Virginia Ali, the young couple who, with a $5,000 loan, opened a half-smoke shop on U Street in 1958. The pair stood by their neighborhood and the city when many others wouldn't and didn't and now Ben's Chili Bowl stands as a living landmark to perseverance. Others take place much more recently but have similar themes, like the story of road warrior Mikala Brennan, who takes to the streets to sell authentic tastes of Hawaii from her aloha-ed-out Hula Girl food truck, or Baked & Wired's Teresa Velazquez, who used her grandmother's rolling pin to make the dough for the first pies she crafted after starting her little indie coffee shop, which now has a huge following.

All the food entrepreneurs featured in *Washington, DC Chef's Table* have built their businesses from the ground up, some more literally than others. Enter James Alefantis of Comet Ping Pong, who did everything from pour the concrete for the pizza oven to fashioning the Ping Pong–like tables in the dining room from reclaimed wood he found, purchased, and carried back to his pizzeria-slash-table-tennis hangout. Or Ben Gilligan, who can take credit for the floors on up at his Columbia Heights restaurant, Room 11.

Like the city itself, there are strong influences from many communities and cultures found in the food that fills this book. This is a town sandwiched between north and south, so the impact of both directions can be seen on just about every menu here. You can indulge in grits one day at Art and Soul and belly up to the Red Hook Lobster Pound truck for a Maine lobster roll the next. Or you can sit down to an artfully prepared dinner at the pretty Blue Duck Tavern and see influences from all points north, south, east, and west. The richness of the Chesapeake Bay watershed fuels many a restaurant regardless of the cuisine or neighborhood, which is why there are an abundance of dishes in DC—and in this book—that center around the fruits of the Bay. The plentiful farmland in nearby Maryland, Virginia, West Virginia, and Pennsylvania also help stock commercial kitchens big and small in this town, to say nothing of the kitchen gardens chefs have lovingly planted in containers, on patios, and in window boxes at their restaurants, turning even the smallest patch of dirt into a blossoming link on the food chain. Watching Michael Costa, head chef at Zaytinya, carefully snip herbs from the blue oversized glazed pots outside the Penn Quarter restaurant stands out as one of my favorite images from this book—one of many, many favorites. Even with downtown traffic flowing through the street behind him and lunch service not far in the distance, his focus on the precise task at hand reminds me over and over again of the care that it takes to make any garden, and any restaurant for that matter, grow. It also for me personifies the small yet significant acts that happen each day within city limits that make this town more than just a place on a postcard or a dot on a map.

The collection of these moments serves as a constant reminder that it is the people who elevate Washington from destination to home and who turn food into meals. These kinds of moments are what make Washington, DC, a place where people live, where people connect, and where people are nourished. It is what makes it home.

A NOTE ABOUT HOW TO USE THIS BOOK:

The recipes in this book range from simple dishes with just a few straightforward ingredients to complex dishes with multiple steps and components. But all are written for the home cook to be made in home kitchens. You can follow the recipes exactly as the chefs have written them or use them as a jumping off point for your own creations by experimenting with substitutions, cooking times, and other tweaks. Make the recipes your own. If it stresses you out to make a stock or sauce from scratch called for in a recipe then you should buy a premade one and enjoy putting the rest of the dish together. Of course, if it stresses you out not to make it from scratch then you should go for it. Whenever possible we recommend using in-season, fresh, locally sourced ingredients along with healthy doses of laughter and good humor. Whether you decide to replicate the dishes teaspoon for teaspoon or to go off-book, do try to remember to have fun along the way—entertaining and eating should be fun. Always taste and season as you cook (and taste and season once more) and try to share the final product with people who make you smile, which makes any recipe turn out better.

After you've done the dishes and wiped down the counters, please tell us about your Chef's Table adventures. We'd love to hear from you. Send us a note about your kitchen successes and your favorite DC dishes. and connect with other Chef's Table fans at facebook.com/DCChefsTable. Here you can keep up-to-date with the chefs we've profiled and see some of our behind-the-scenes photos. You can even post your own pictures of Chef's Table dishes you've made at home and tell us about your stove-side escapades. We look forward to hearing from you.

Bon appétit. Itadakimasu. Bonum appetitionem. Prijatnovo appetita. Guten appétit. Que aproveche. Bete-avon. Buon appetito. Jal meokkesseumnida. Sihk faahn. Bil hana wish shifa. Kalí óreksi. Smakelijk eten . . . Well, you get the idea . . .

Art and Soul

415 New Jersey Avenue NW
Washington, DC 20001
(202) 393-7777
ARTANDSOULDC.COM
Chef/Owner: Art Smith
Executive Chef: Wes Morton

Chef Wes Morton has always known where his food comes from. As a boy growing up in Lafayette, Louisiana, if he wanted fish, he went fishing. If he wanted meat, he went hunting. And, if you wanted it all cooked to Southern perfection, you went to his family table on Sundays for the weekly feast prepared by his grandmother. A young Morton often served as sous-chef for those beloved meals.

"I grew up in a family surrounded by food and cooks," says Morton, who was drawn to the kitchen as far back as he can remember. "We have pictures of me helping with the cooking when I was maybe five or six years old."

These early memories continue to guide his outlook on food and work. Morton remains committed to using local ingredients whenever possible. He embraces the farm-to-table movement not just as a way to put the best food on the table but also as a vehicle to put money back in the local economy. "A sense of community comes from knowing where goods comes from," he explains.

There also is no doubt where his cooking sense comes from. Like Chef Art Smith, Morton has been shaped by the tastes, techniques, and flavors of the South. This recipe for shrimp and grits is a perfect case in point. Grits, practically required eating below the Mason-Dixon Line, are prepared and served with a more modern, upscale dining twist at the popular Capitol Hill restaurant. He often serves them with crème fraîche and pickled okra.

Grits demand time and patience. Lots of time and patience. While you'd be hard-pressed to find a Washingtonian who isn't short on both, Morton does ask that you resist the temptation of instant grits. They truly aren't as good and, no self-respecting Southerner will take you seriously if you go the quickie route. Slow and steady are the art and the soul of the grits race.

Shrimp & Grits

SERVES 1 WITH ENOUGH GRITS TO SPARE

1 cup coarse organic white grits

1 cup fine organic white grits

8 cups water

Salt to taste

5 each 21–25 count fresh shrimp, shells removed and deveined

1 tablespoon oil

1 ounce andouille sausage, cut into half-inch cubes

2 tablespoons crème fraîche

1 tablespoon Parmesan cheese, grated

2 tablespoons chives, shaved

1 ounce butter

Lemon juice to taste

Worcestershire sauce to taste

Mix coarse and fine grits together in a mixing bowl. In a saucepot, add water with room to spare and bring to a boil. Slowly add the grits to the pot of boiling water while whisking vigorously. Allow grits to come to a slow simmer and continue to whisk. Whisk every 10 minutes until they become tender, which should take between four and five hours. Add salt to taste. Put the cooked grits in a container and set aside for later.

Season the shrimp with salt on both sides and set aside.

Bring a dry sauté pan to a light smoke and then add just enough oil to barely the coat pan. Add andouille sausage and cook until all sides are caramelized. Drain the sausage on paper towels. Save pan with the oil.

Meanwhile, add one cup of cooked grits to a small saucepot. Add crème fraîche, Parmesan cheese, chives, and then salt to taste. Bring to a simmer and whisk to keep a smooth consistency.

Take the pan used to cook the andouille, put it back on the stove, and bring it back to a smoke. Add shrimp and cook them until they are caramelized on both sides. Allow shrimp to cook all the way through, lowering the heat as needed. Drain the shrimp on paper towels.

Pour the oil out of the pan. Add 2 tablespoons of water and the butter. Allow pan sauce to reduce until slightly thickened. Add lemon juice, Worcestershire sauce, and salt as needed.

Spoon the grits in to the middle of a small serving bowl and place the shrimp on top of the grits. Add cooked andouille to the sauce left in the pan and then pour the mixture over shrimp and serve.

BAKED & WIRED

1052 THOMAS JEFFERSON STREET NW
WASHINGTON, DC 20007
(202) 333-2500
BAKEDANDWIRED.COM
CO-OWNER: TERESA VELAZQUEZ

Until I met Teresa Velazquez I thought baking love into your food was something relegated to stories of the animated sort. But after spending some time with the sweet-as-sugar Baked & Wired co-owner I am convinced that she does just that. It's the only way I can think to explain how her to-die-for cookies, bars, and buttercream-topped treats defy the conventional boundaries of deliciousness. That and her extraordinary talent and devotion to her craft.

"After a 16-hour day, when it's 3:30 in the morning and I still have two more trays of cupcakes to frost, I know I could just rush through it and be done," she tells. "Then I stop and think about someone opening up the package and seeing it for the first time and I know I need to make it look great. It's very gratifying making something that makes someone happy."

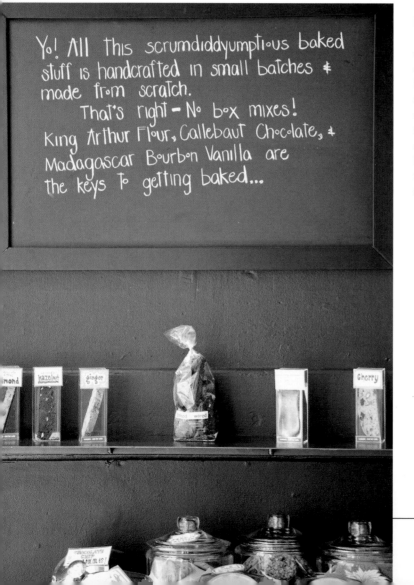

Velazquez's pies make her—and her customers—especially happy. The Columbus-born mom of two young adults learned the art of pie-making from her grandmother and until very recently even used her grandma's beloved cherrywood rolling pin in her Baked & Wired kitchen. When Velazquez first opened her hip Georgetown coffee and bakeshop, she would put out several of her fruit-filled creations each morning only to find them untouched at the end of the day. Thankfully she didn't let that deter her from making more. Slowly but surely, the word got out and slices started to sell. Today, more than eleven years after she opened the shop with her husband Tony, at closing time it's only the crumbs that are left.

Pie-making at home doesn't need to be an exacting, precise, or stressful exercise, Velazquez reassures me. "The Martha Stewarts of the world have psyched people out that they can't make pie," she says explaining that she doesn't use cutouts or other fancy techniques but instead uses her fingers and thumbs to shape her delicious and pretty pies. "Something about the rustic look is comforting," she shares. "And, beautiful."

While you don't need elaborate equipment, Velazquez does advise investing in a good rolling pin and a pastry cloth. Improvising will compromise the coveted final product. "Go spend $30 on a pastry cloth and a rolling pin," she says. "It makes a huge difference."

She also advises pie newbies, along with everyone else attempting her cream peach pie for the first time, to have your dough be on the wetter side. When the dough is too dry, it cracks and will be challenging to manipulate, which makes the likelihood of getting frustrated during the process increase. If you find your dough is too dry, you can add a couple of teaspoons of water to moisten it up.

"If it doesn't turn out the way you wanted what really is lost?" she asks. "Two cups of flour and a cup of Crisco. Throw it out and make another."

PINK RIDER

You know you've turned down the right street toward Baked & Wired when you spy the hot-pink bicycle that stands in front of the popular Georgetown hangout. The pretty-in-pink bike in question, like so much of the rest of the space, comes from the design imagination of Teresa's husband Tony, an architect and co-owner of the indie coffeeshop. On a whim he spray-painted an old bike that belonged to their now-adult daughter when she was about ten years old. Tony added the basket on the handlebars that often holds flowers, and a bubblegum-colored Baked & Wired landmark was born.

CREAM PEACH PIE

MAKES 1 PIE

For the crust (for double crust):

3 cups unbleached all-purpose flour

1 teaspoon kosher salt

1 cup Butter Crisco shortening

⅔ cup plus 2 tablespoons of cold water

For the filling:

¾ cup sugar, plus extra to sprinkle on strips

3 tablespoons flour

⅛ teaspoon salt

½ cup heavy cream

1 whole egg

1 egg yolk (save egg white for top of crust)

5 to 6 fresh peaches (can also use frozen, thawed peaches), peeled and cut into 6 slices each

1 teaspoon pure vanilla extract

Cinnamon

To prepare the crust: Preheat your oven to 400°F. To make the crust, whisk flour and salt, and add shortening. Work with fingers until it forms pea-size balls. You can work the flour and shortening until you do not see any white flour. Add cold water by sprinkling over flour.

At this point you do not want to work with the mixture much, just toss it until it comes together. Form two balls. You can make one ball larger than the other and use the larger one for the bottom crust so you have more to work with.

Let dough sit in a bowl with a damp, cold towel on top of the bowl for 10 minutes so it can rest. A pastry cloth or thin kitchen towel on top works best.

Take your ball of dough and flatten it out like a patty to 1-inch thick. Make sure to tighten around the outside edge and seal the dough so it does not crack open when rolling out. Roll from the middle out, and roll in all directions to create your circle. Place in the bottom of a glass Pyrex pie dish, gently pushing dough down the sides.

To prepare the filling: Combine sugar, flour, salt, cream, egg, egg yolk, and vanilla. Whisk together. Lay peaches in bottom crust. Pour mixture over peaches (you may not need all the liquid to cover them). Sprinkle with cinnamon. Roll out other ball of dough. Cut eight ¾-inch strips to use as a lattice top. Place lattice strips on top of filling and weave the strips over and under each other to create the pattern.

To seal the lattice strips to the bottom of the crust, put a dab of water under each strip of dough and push down on bottom crust to seal. Tear away all but ¾ inch of extra dough from top and bottom crusts.

Fold the hanging dough from your under crust and lattice strips under itself so it sits on the lip of the pie dish. Using your thumb and index finger of both hands, bring fingers together, and pinch to get decorative edge. You will have quite a bit of dough left over after making crust—remaining dough can be frozen and used later on.

Using a basting brush, brush some of the egg white on to the lattice strips. Sprinkle sugar on the strips.

Bake for 1 hour. Depending on your oven, you may need to put a crust ring over the edge of the pie to prevent the crust from getting too brown.

Bandolero

3241 M Street NW
Washington, DC 20007
(202) 625-4488
BANDOLERODC.COM
Partner/Chef: Mike Isabella; Mixologist: Sam Babcock

You can hear the smile behind Chef Mike Isabella's words when he starts talking about Mexican food. The happy inflection punctuates the conversation as the former *Top Chef* contestant declares his love of the Latin food culture and a cheery tone takes hold when he talks about its array of fresh flavor combinations or its intriguing range of spices. "It's the food I enjoy eating, it's the food I enjoy cooking, and it's the food I enjoy playing around with in the kitchen," says Isabella who recently opened Bandolero in Georgetown as something of a modern Mexican food playground for both customers and chef.

A Mexican food playground against a slightly dark backdrop, that is. Isabella decided to use *Day of the Dead* as the inspiration for Bandolero's interior. Dark strokes in the decor include old fencing that once stood guard at an actual cemetery, dim lighting, and animal skulls on the walls. Although the creepy chic decor takes Bandolero out of the running for most toddler birthday parties or the next church ladies' lunch, it does set the tone for fun while not falling into amusement park ride territory.

When it came time for the food, Isabella resisted the urge to go dark there, too. Instead he opted for a menu that reflects what he likes most when he goes out to enjoy one of his favorite food genres. "When I go to a Mexican restaurant I always get a margarita when I sit down and then I order some kind of taco," he says. So at Bandolero the taco choices are plentiful and the margaritas flow on tap. The restaurant also has a fabulous cocktail list.

Other takes on traditional dishes round out the offerings, including these empanadas. Isabella promises the empanadas are easy to re-create at home and notes that dissolving the sugar in water helps give the dough its color and flavor. He also stresses the importance of keeping the butter very cold when you make the dough and recommends having it do a stint in the freezer before you use it. The chilled butter makes the dough a nice and flaky consistency and even an old cemetery gate can't block the light out of that.

THE FAMILY TABLE

Mike Isabella's father-in-law, Charlie Nemeth, handcrafted all the tables at both Bandolero and Graffiato, the chef's first DC restaurant. Nemeth, a woodworker by hobby not trade, learned the art from his father. "I started working with wood when I was around twelve or thirteen years old," says Nemeth, who created the Bandolero tables from bamboo wood and also made the wine credenza at Graffiato. "My interest in woodworking came from my dad. My dad always had some project he was working on for a neighbor or a friend. I helped him and learned from that time I spent with him."

Empanada with Roasted Poblano Peppers, Corn & Jack Cheese

MAKES 6

For the filling:

2 poblano peppers, lightly oiled with extra-virgin
    olive oil and seasoned with salt

3 tablespoons canola oil

½ cup finely diced yellow onion

¼ cup minced garlic

1½ cup fresh sweet corn

1 cup Monterey Jack cheese

½ cup sour cream

2 tablespoons finely chopped cilantro

1 teaspoon ground cumin

1 teaspoon kosher salt

Empanada dough (recipe to follow)

6 cups canola oil for frying

For the empanada dough:

¾ cup warm water

¼ cup white granulated sugar

¼ teaspoon kosher salt

2 cups all-purpose flour

4 ounces unsalted butter; chilled and
    cut into ½-inch cubes

To prepare the filling: Preheat the oven broiler on high. Arrange the poblano peppers on a baking sheet and place under your broiler. Broil for 5–6 minutes on all sides. This will take approximately 20–25 minutes. The skins will become charred and the flesh soft.

Remove the baking sheet from the oven. Place the peppers in a glass bowl and cover tightly with plastic wrap. Set aside for 20 minutes to cool.

Once cooled, remove peppers from the bowl and cut each in half. Peel the skin off and remove the ribs and seeds. Dice into ¼-inch pieces and set aside.

Heat the canola oil in a large sauté pan over medium heat. Sweat the onions for 4–5 minutes or until soft and translucent. Add the garlic and sweat for 1–2 minutes longer. Then add the corn and cook for 3–4 minutes, stirring often. If color begins to form, add a small amount of water to prevent burning.

Remove from heat and add to a large mixing bowl. Add in the peppers, Jack cheese, sour cream, cilantro, cumin, and salt. Stir well to combine all ingredients. Refrigerate until ready to use.

To prepare the empanada dough: Combine the water, sugar, and salt in a small bowl. Stir until sugar and salt are fully dissolved and then place the mixture in the freezer for 8–10 minutes or until just chilled. Add the flour and butter to a food processor fitted with the dough blade. Turn on the food processor and blend for approximately

30–40 seconds or until a course crumble forms. Keeping the food processor on, add the water a tablespoon at a time. The ingredients will start to pull away from the sides of the processor and a dough mass will begin to form. This will take between 30 to 60 seconds. Remove the dough and form into a smooth ball. Wrap tightly in plastic wrap and place in the refrigerator for at least 20 minutes.

Divide empanada dough into six even portions. On a lightly floured surface roll the dough out into ¼-inch-thick circles. On one half of each circle, evenly distribute the cheese mixture. Make sure to leave ¼ inch around the edge for sealing. Fold over each empanada, creating half circles. Starting at one end, seal the edges by pressing with a fork so no filling will spill out. Refrigerate uncovered for 20 minutes to allow them to set.

Heat the canola oil for frying in an electric deep fryer to 350°F. If you do not have an electric fryer, use a heavy-bottom pot and a candy thermometer to keep track of the oil's temperature. It is important to make sure to monitor temperature of the oil because it will drop in between frying.

Once oil is to temperature, gently add each empanada one at a time. You may need to fry in batches depending on the size of your fryer. Fry for 4–5 minutes or until golden brown on both sides. Remove from oil and drain on a paper towel.

To serve: Transfer to a serving platter or individual plates and serve immediately.

City of Gold Cocktail

MAKES 1 COCKTAIL

1½ ounces reposado tequila
1 ounce Cardamaro
½ ounce St-Germain liqueur
½ ounce 5-Spice Syrup (see recipe below)
¾ ounce fresh lemon juice
Freshly grated cinnamon for garnish

Combine all the ingredients in a cocktail shaker with ice. Strain into a chilled coupe/stemmed cocktail glass.

Garnish with a touch of freshly grated cinnamon.

5-Spice Syrup

2 cups water
2 cinnamon sticks
7 whole cloves
2 whole star anise
1 tablespoon fresh ginger, peeled and grated
3 black peppercorns lightly crushed
2 cups sugar

Combine the water and all five spices in a saucepan. Bring to a boil, cover, and let simmer for 30 minutes.

Remove from heat, strain out solids, then combine liquid with sugar and whisk until dissolved.

Pour liquid into a container and chill in the refrigerator. The syrup can keep for up to two weeks.

Beau Thai

1700 New Jersey Avenue NW
Washington, DC 20001
(202) 536-5636 ·
BEAUTHAIDC.COM
Chef/Co-Owner: Aschara
Vigsittaboot
Co-Owner: Ralph Brabham

Aschara Vigsittaboot stands beneath a black-and-white photo of a far-off house. It's the house in Bangkok that her father built, the house where her mother still lives, the house where many years ago she perfected the art of Thai cooking.

"There used to be nothing around it but now it's a very crowded area," Vigsittaboot says, her eyes cast up toward the picture, one of several old family photos that decorate the walls of the Shaw eatery. On the other side of the restaurant is a photo of Vigsittaboot's mother, whose beauty and glamour give her the appearance of a Hollywood starlet from days gone by. The captivating photo of Vigsittaboot's mother is not the only homage to her at Beau Thai. The dishes, many done in the Southern style of Thai cooking that filled the Vigsittaboot house on the wall, are ones that have been passed down from mother to child. Her Yum Beef is one of those recipes that Vigsittaboot learned to cook from her mother, and the version that she serves at the restaurant is somewhat specific to Bangkok.

"All of our curries here are made from scratch," she says. "Everything we use here is fresh. Pre-peeled garlic or store-bought lime juice never tastes or smells as good as the hand-peeled and hand-squeezed stuff."

She does point out that the vegetables and garnishes in the recipe do not need to be strictly replicated when you make her Yum Beef at home. She likes to change it up, too. Sometimes she includes carrots, sometimes she does not. The kinds of onions she uses can vary a bit based on what is fresh and available. You should also feel free to experiment this way without worrying about losing the integrity of the dish, she says.

When you order the Yum Beef at the restaurant, try to snag the table against the purple accent wall punctuated with an old photo of Aschara Vigsittaboot herself as a college student. She is holding an elaborately folded banana leaf and wearing a long, striped silk skirt, traditional Thai clothing, she explains. The shot was taken during *Loi Krathong,* a celebration that takes place during a full moon in the fall. The leaves, often decorated with flowers and candles, are floated on the water. In this photo, a smiling young Vigsittaboot holds the lotus-shaped leaf before it joins others atop the water. A moment in time that now always is part of the present at Beau Thai.

Yum Beef Salad

SERVES 6

1 pound flank steak

2 cups soy sauce

2 cups vegetable oil

6 cherry tomatoes sliced in half

1 cucumber, peeled, sliced in half, lengthwise, and then sliced into ¼-inch slivers

2 medium shallots, sliced

½ medium white onion, sliced into ¼ inch pieces

1 small carrot, peeled and juliened

2 tablespoons nam prik pao (Thai chili paste in oil —sometimes called Thai chili jam—available at Asian markets and online)

2 tablespoons fish sauce

4 tablespoons lime juice

½ tablespoon sugar

Garnish of green onion, sliced, and cilantro

Marinate the flank steak for at least two hours before cooking it by placing the steak in a baking dish, pouring the soy sauce and vegetable oil over it, and then placing it in refrigerator to marinate. After the steak has marinated, grill the meat to the desired temperature (at Beau Thai the dish is served medium rare) and slice into bite-sized pieces.

Mix vegetables together with flank steak.

To make the dressing, combine the nam prik pao, fish sauce, lime juice, and sugar. Pour the dressing over vegetables and meat and toss.

Garnish with green onion and cilantro.

BEN'S CHILI BOWL

1213 U STREET NW
WASHINGTON, DC 20009
(202) 667-0909
BENSCHILIBOWL.COM
OWNERS: THE ALI FAMILY

Sonya Ali holds up a plain brown bag. "It's our secret blend," she says of the unassuming paper sack containing the spices her family has been using for more than fifty years to make the famous chili at Ben's Chili Bowl. A secret that the family guards with pride and love even after all these years, much to the delight of anyone who has lined up for one of Ben's half-smokes at two in the morning.

The Ben's Chili Bowl story begins in 1958, when Ben and Virginia Ali started the U Street chili dog shop with $5,000. It was in the heyday of the U Street corridor, known back then as "Black Broadway." The greats like Ella Fitzgerald, Duke Ellington, Miles Davis, Cab Calloway, and Nat King Cole played the clubs that lined the street and often hung out in the neighborhood at places like Ben's. In 1968, the painful and tragic news of Dr. Martin Luther King Jr.'s assassination broke. In the days following his murder, rioting broke out. Much of Washington was forced to shut down, but Ben's Chili Bowl got special permission to remain open past curfew to provide food and shelter to those trying to restore order. The years following the riots were trying ones for the once-thriving neighborhood, but Ben's remained at 1213 U through it all.

A recent rebirth has brought new life to the corridor and a new generation of Ben's fans through its doors. The restaurant—still with its original booths, stools, and counter—remains at the same spot where it stood in 1958. Ben's also has stands at Nationals Park and has taken over the space next to it to open Ben's Next Door. But two things haven't changed: the chili-topped half-smokes and the Alis' dedication to family, the business, and the neighborhood. Today Ben and Virginia's sons and their wives run the iconic restaurant. Ben passed away in 2009 but Virginia still pops in from time to time to chat with customers and check on the DC food landmark she started all those years ago.

COLESLAW

MAKES ABOUT 15 SERVINGS

1 large head of cabbage (about 2 pounds with dark green leaves for added color)
4 medium carrots, peeled
2 cups mayonnaise
¼ cup sugar
⅛ cup cider vinegar
Pinch of salt
Dash of vanilla extract

Shred the cabbage and carrots to a fine consistency. Combine all the ingredients and continue to season to your taste preference. At the restaurant, the coleslaw is served sweet and with a little bit of tang.

TOP DOGS

On January 10, 2009, just ten days before he took the oath of office, President Barack Obama stopped by Ben's Chili Bowl for lunch. It was a thrilling day for the Ali family, but it was not the first time the family served a famous customer. A long list of celebrities, entertainers, politicians, and heads of state have eaten at the iconic U Street restaurant. Among those who have bellied up to the counter at Ben's Chili Bowl are Bono, Ted Koppel, Chris Tucker, Chubby Checker, Supreme Court Justice Elena Kagan, and French President Nicolas Sarkozy. Bill Cosby, who courted his wife at Ben's in the 1960s, has a half-smoke named for him and for years a sign on the wall declared that Bill Cosby was the only person who got to eat for free at Ben's Chili Bowl. In 2008, the sign was changed to say "Bill Cosby and the Obama family."

BISTRO BIS

15 E STREET NW
WASHINGTON, DC 20001
(202) 661-2700
BISTROBIS.COM
CHEF/CO-OWNER: JEFFREY BUBEN
CO-OWNER: SALLIE BUBEN
CHEF DE CUISINE: JOE HARRAN

Hotel George helped the DC lodging scene leave its colonial reproduction image behind when it opened as the city's first truly contemporary boutique hotel in 1998. With its über-modern decor and Andy Warhol–inspired presidential Pop Art, it was abundantly clear this wasn't your typical beige-and-brown chain hotel and, because of that, your typical hotel restaurant just wouldn't do here. Enter Sallie and Jeffrey Buben, the husband-and-wife team behind Vidalia, who were brought in to help find the right restaurant for the Capitol Hill hotel.

"After some time, we, along with the Hotel George, realized that the answer was right in front of us," says Buben, who ultimately wound up as the hotel's culinary tenant when he opened the doors to Bistro Bis at the funky hotel. "And it's been a fifteen-year relationship."

And counting.

The upscale contemporary French restaurant housed at Hotel George continues to attract Inside-the-Beltway power players, tourists, and locals-in-the-know with its solid reputation and modern bistro-style menu. Buben's recipes, like this one for Citrus-Cured Salmon with Tartare of Spring Vegetables, continue to please Bistro Bis's myriad customers.

Chef de Cuisine Joe Harran cannot stress enough the importance of stocking your kitchen with the proper tools before you start the prep for this dish, or any dish for that matter. Topping his list are a set of quality knives (he prefers Japanese-made ones like Global, Masahiro, or Mac), a mandoline, and a microplane for zesting. His other advice: Taste, taste, taste.

"If it tastes good to you, chances are your guests will agree," he says.

Citrus-Cured Salmon with Tartare of Spring Vegetables

SERVES 6

For the salmon:

1 teaspoon orange zest, finely grated

1 teaspoon lemon zest, finely grated

1 teaspoon lime zest, finely grated

1 teaspoon grapefruit zest, finely grated

¼ cup kosher salt

2 tablespoons granulated sugar

2 tablespoons freshly ground black pepper

6 (3-ounce) salmon fillets (skin and pin bones removed)

For the vegetables:

¼ cup diced fennel bulb

¼ cup peeled and diced carrots

¼ cup peeled and diced small turnips

¼ cup diced zucchini

¼ cup diced yellow squash

1 cup fresh shelled English peas

6 spears asparagus, peeled and diced

½ cup fresh shelled fava beans (outer skin removed)

1 tomato, peeled, seeded, and diced

2 tablespoons flat-leaf parsley, chopped

2 tablespoons chives, minced

1 teaspoon fresh tarragon, chopped

2 tablespoons fresh basil, chopped

For the vinaigrette:

2 tablespoons minced shallots

½ teaspoon minced garlic

1 tablespoon Dijon mustard

⅛ cup champagne vinegar

⅔ cup extra-virgin olive oil

Salt and freshly ground pepper to taste

To prepare the salmon: Start by combining all the seasonings together in a bowl. Cut six pieces of aluminum foil larger than the salmon fillets so the fish can be wrapped like packages in the foil. Distribute half the seasonings evenly on the bottoms of the six pieces of foil. Place the salmon fillets in the center of the foil and top with the remaining seasonings, evenly distributed. Wrap tightly like a package and refrigerate for 3 hours. Unwrap the packages and wipe off the seasoning from the fillets and put them back in the refrigerator until ready to serve.

To prepare the vegetables: Bring a large pot of salted water to a boil over a high heat. Cook each type of vegetable (except the tomato) one at a time for 1 ½ minutes each, removing them from the water with a slotted spoon and placing them in a bowl of ice water. Drain the vegetables in a colander and then on paper towels. Set aside.

To prepare the vinaigrette: Whisk the shallots, garlic, mustard, and vinegar together in a large bowl, adding the olive oil in a thin stream. Season with the salt and freshly ground pepper. Add the cooked vegetables, tomatoes, and herbs. Mix gently.

To serve: Place a mound of vegetables in the center of a plate. Slice salmon thinly across the grain and fan the salmon slices over the vegetables. Drizzle with extra-virgin olive oil.

THE BLIND DOG CAFÉ AT DARNELL'S

BLACK STRAP BAKERY
944 FLORIDA AVENUE NW
WASHINGTON, DC 20001
(202) 290-2865
BLINDDOGCAFE.COM
BAKER AND BLACK STRAP BAKERY OWNER: GREER ANN GILCHRIST
BLIND DOG CAFE AT DARNELL'S CO-OWNERS: CULLEN GILCHRIST,
NOAH KARESH, AND JONAS SINGER

When Greer Ann Gilchrist boarded the bus from Boston to DC, she took one seat for herself and the one next to her for her KitchenAid mixer. Gilchrist packed her treasured pale pink mixer, a birthday gift from her mother, in its own suitcase for her move to DC. You can see her using it just about every day in the small kitchen area in the front section of Blind Dog Cafe, a pop-up neighborhood coffee shop housed in Darnell's Bar on Florida Avenue off U Street.

"It was a gift from my mom when I turned twenty-two," says Gilchrist who credits her mom as her biggest baking influence. "It felt so important when I got it. I love that thing."

Gilchrist is responsible for all the yummy cookies, scones, croissants, muffins, and other goodies served at Blind Dog Cafe. In what can best be described as the matryoshka dolls of start-up businesses, Gilchrist runs the Black Strap Bakery, the pop-up bakery within the pop-up cafe, Blind Dog, which is housed in the bar. No word yet on whether or not there is a pop up microbrewery or pool hall lurking anywhere within these nesting businesses but the cafe has hosted other limited short-term endeavors like a local artisanal ice cream tasting and a clothing swap.

The cafe's name is a nod to the sightless pup belonging to one of the three owners, Jonas Singer. Another member of the trio, Cullen Gilchrist, a line cook at Ardeo + Bardeo, is Greer's brother, and the third partner, Noah Karesh, grew up in Chevy Chase. Creating a local place with great cappuccino, comfy couches, and a cozy living room vibe brought the three together. It is an experiment rich with mismatched furniture and free Wi-Fi that seems to be working. Gilchrist's soft chocolate chip cookies, which she makes with the goal of chocolate in each and every bite, seem to be helping the endeavors move more away from pop-up and more toward sit-down-and-stay-a-while-longer.

TAN BUTTER

One bite of baker Greer Gilchrist's heavenly chocolate chip cookies lets you know she has a magic touch, and Gilchrist points to the creaming of the butter and sugar as the most significant step in moving from good to great on the cookie meter. "When you cream the butter and sugar together, it should change color from brown and white to tan," she shares. "Otherwise the sugar is not fully incorporated and the texture of the cookie will be grainy." It can take up to ten minutes to get the color and mixture just right so Gilchrist reminds you to be patient. The final product will be worth it.

GALLETAS DE CHOCOLATE DE AMOR

MAKES 12 OVERSIZE COOKIES OR
24 STANDARD-SIZE COOKIES

2 cups all-purpose flour
1 teaspoon baking soda
1¼ teaspoons salt
½ cup (1 stick) unsalted butter, room temperature
¾ cup brown sugar
½ cup white sugar
1 egg
1 teaspoon vanilla
2 cups chocolate chips—dark and milk
    (can also use chocolate chunks)

Preheat oven to 350°F. Line a baking sheet with parchment paper (alternatively you can also use a good nonstick tray). In a bowl, combine flour, baking soda, and salt. With a mixer beat butter and sugars together until fully blended and the mixture is tan in color. Add egg. Add vanilla. Slowly add the flour mixture. Add the chocolate chips.

Form the dough into balls and place on the lined baking sheets. At Blind Dog, Greer uses an ice cream scoop to create the oversize cookies she bakes, but she says you can make them any size you wish as long as you leave about 2 inches between the cookies so they don't conjoin as they bake.

Bake for 10 minutes.

BLUE DUCK TAVERN

1201 24TH STREET NW
WASHINGTON, DC 20037
(202) 419-6755
BLUEDUCKTAVERN.COM
EXECUTIVE CHEF: SEBASTIEN ARCHAMBAULT
PASTRY CHEF: PETER BRETT

Chef Sebastien Archambault takes a seat in the oversized black rocking chair near the entrance of the Blue Duck Tavern, leans back, and flashes a playful smile. The executive chef is at home and happy here and his level of comfort comes through in the cooking he does at the light-filled restaurant with the open kitchen and simple yet pretty contemporary Shaker design.

The Texas-born chef who moved to France as a young boy seamlessly took over the lovely restaurant housed at the Park Hyatt not too long ago. He has added his own touches and influences, creating a kind of 2.0 version of the original menu while keeping favorites like the much-beloved duck-fat fries in intact. His Poached Egg with Field Mushroom Ragout and *Foie Gras* shows the kind of dishes he has brought to the menu, built around fresh flavors, local ingredients, and reimagined American cuisine.

The Blue Duck's pastry chef Peter Brett exhibits a similar level of ease and expertise with the pastry program at the West End eatery, widely pointed to for serving some of the best restaurant desserts in town. He too sources his ingredients from a group of hand-picked suppliers. For the BDT Strawberry Shortcake, he only uses strawberries that are red throughout and the payoff can be savored in every last bite of the divine final product. Not ordering some of his homemade ice cream to accompany it can be considered an act of subversion. Try the strawberry ice cream when it too is in season. It may even contain some of the fruit from the patch in the garden that frames the outdoor patio.

Poached Egg with Field Mushroom Ragout & Foie Gras

SERVES 4

For the mushroom ragout:

¼ pound shiitake mushrooms

¼ pound oyster mushrooms

¼ cup blended oil

1 garlic clove

fresh sprig of thyme, which seasonally can be found
growing in Blue Duck Tavern's outdoor herb garden)

¼ cup heavy cream

3 ounces mushroom ragout

1 fresh egg

½ ounce foie gras terrine

1 slice country top bread

1 teaspoon butter

Black pepper

3 shaved black truffles

Special equipment: A small cast-iron pot (an
individual-size Le Creuset pot works well)

To prepare the mushroom ragout: Preheat the oven to 350°F. Wash and dice the mushrooms. Mix the mushrooms with the oil, garlic, and thyme. Place on a sheet pan and cook in the oven for 10 minutes. Remove and let mushrooms cool. Once cooled, chop the mushrooms. Add the cream and cook for 10 minutes. Cool down and store in refrigerator.

To assemble: Warm the mushroom ragout and place into a small cast-iron pot. Crack the egg on top of the ragout and then place into a double boiler and cover. Cook until the egg is medium, and then remove the pot from the double boiler. Cut the foie gras into a half moon and place next to the egg.

Toast the bread and spread the butter on top. Cut the bread into 4 batonette pieces and stack next to the cast-iron pot. Season with cracked black pepper and black truffles. Serve.

BDT Strawberry Shortcake

SERVES 8–10

6 ounces cake flour

6 ounces all-purpose flour

¼ cup sugar

2 teaspoons baking powder

2 teaspoons salt

½ teaspoon baking soda

4 ounces (1 stick) unsalted butter

1 cup buttermilk

½ cup heavy cream

Grated rind of 1 orange

For the strawberries:

2 pints fresh strawberries

¼ cup granulated sugar

2 tablespoons Grand Marnier (optional)

2 cups heavy cream

¼ cup confectioners' sugar

Preheat the oven to 400°F. Mix all the dry ingredients. Cut the butter into the flour with a pastry blender or the tips of your fingers so it resembles coarse meal. Stir in the buttermilk, cream, and orange rind quickly, being careful not to overmix.

Portion into 3-inch dessert rings on a greased cookie sheet using an ice cream scoop.

Bake until browned and cooked through, about 15 minutes. Cool.

Wash, hull, and slice 2 pints of fresh strawberries. Sprinkle with ¼ cup sugar (or to taste) and 2 tablespoons of Grand Marnier (optional). Whip 2 cups heavy cream with ¼ cup confectioners sugar.

Split the biscuits in half and fill with the marinated strawberries. Top with whipped cream.

SEALED WITH A CAKE:

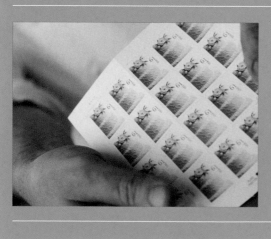

Thanks to Chef Peter Brett, the three-tiered wedding cake on the US Postal Service's special wedding stamp looks good enough to eat. The Blue Duck Tavern pastry chef designed, baked, and decorated the ivory wedding cake topped with white roses that now adorns many an invitation. Brett has even had the experience of being greeted by the photo of his beautiful cake beneath the postmark when opening his own mailbox at home. Local photographer Renée Comet captured the image of the cake used on the stamp, which is part of the post office's popular wedding series.

BOQUERIA DUPONT CIRCLE

1837 M STREET NW
WASHINGTON, DC 20036
(202) 558-9545
BOQUERIADC.COM
EXECUTIVE CHEF: MARC VIDAL
OWNER: YANN DE ROCHEFORT

When I picture Chef Marc Vidal's family tree, I imagine it planted right alongside a restaurant, providing shade to what can easily be considered his family's business. Growing up in Barcelona, Vidal's grandfather owned a restaurant and later on his mother and aunt bought an eatery of their own called Roca, where they served traditional Spanish dishes for twenty years. Roca was Vidal's home—and kitchen—away from home.

"In the morning I would go with my mom to help her open," he happily recalls what was the daily routine from the time he was six years old until he was sixteen. "I would make coffee and bread and Spanish omelets. Then after school I would go back to be with my mom and help some more."

Vidal started culinary school at sixteen and his career path took him from Spain to France to Miami—with a few other stops along the way. From Miami he moved up north to Boqueria, first in New York and then here, bringing with him a creative spin on the beloved Spanish cuisine inspired by the kind of cooking his mom and grandfather used to do back home.

The Fideua Negra served at the Dupont Circle restaurant is one of those dishes. "My family ate it all the time on Sundays by the beach," he tells. "This version is like the classic dish but with squid ink."

When attempting his recipe at home, Vidal stresses the importance of letting the *sofrito* cook for a long, long time. The recipe calls for two hours but if you can let it go for six hours it will be that much better and well worth the sweat equity and time, he tells. The chef also wants the home cook to know that a paella pan really is necessary to make this dish, but if you want to use a premade lobster or fish stock you can, although, of course, homemade is almost always better and will make the dish that much more flavorful. If you can find a beach to stare at as you eat, it's a pretty safe bet it will taste even better.

FIDEUA NEGRA

SQUID INK FIDEO

SERVES 1

For the lobster stock:*

2 lobster heads, cut in half

2 tablespoons canola oil

½ Spanish onion, chopped

1 carrot, peeled and finely chopped

2 garlic cloves, skin on

1 leek, finely chopped

1 teaspoon sweet paprika

3 plum tomatoes, roughly chopped

½ cup brandy

½ cup white wine

Water to cover (about 2 quarts)

1 tablespoon tomato paste

4 tablespoons squid ink

*Store-bought lobster or fish stock can be
    used instead of homemade.

For the sofrito:

Olive oil, a small amount to coat the pan

2 onions

2 garlic clove

2 tomatoes, grated

1 large sepia (cuttlefish) cut in ½-inch dice

3 ruby red shrimp

1 tablespoon sofrito

1 cup small fideo noodles (pre-toasted in the oven
    at 350°F for about 7–10 minutes until golden brown)

12 ounces lobster stock*

Salt to taste

4 manila clams

Olive oil for drizzling

1 tablespoon garlic aioli (store-bought is fine)

Chopped chives for garnish

Special equipment: Paella pan

To prepare the lobster stock: Sauté the
lobster heads in a large pot with the canola
oil over medium heat. Cook until the lobster is
caramelized. Remove the lobster from the pot
and set aside.

In the same pot, sweat the onions, carrots, garlic
and leeks for 10 minutes over medium heat. Add
the sweet paprika and sweat without burning for
30 seconds, until fragrant. Add the tomatoes and
cook for 5 minutes. Add the brandy and flambé.
Add the white wine and cook until reduced by half.

Place the lobster back into the pot, add water
and bring to a boil. Let simmer for 1 hour. Remove
from the heat and let infuse for 2 hours. After two
hours, strain through a fine chinoise. Mix the stock
with the squid ink and stir until it is combined.

To prepare the sofrito: Start by heating the olive
oil in a pan over medium heat. Cut the onions
and garlic in small dice and cook in the pan until
translucent. Add the tomatoes and continue to
cook for 30 minutes. Add the sepia and reduce
the heat to low, cooking for approximately 2 more
hours until the sofrito is caramelized and has a
consistency of marmalade. Cook uncovered.

To prepare the fideua: Preheat the oven to 450°F. In a paella pan, sear the shrimp on both sides and set aside. Add the sofrito to the pan and sauté for 1 minute. Add the fideo noodles and stir to combine with the sofrito. Add the boiling stock and salt to taste. Cook for about 5 minutes on high and then place the manila clams and the shrimp on top. Place in the oven at 450°F for about 5 more minutes. Remove when fideos are crispy on top and the liquid is gone. Drizzle with olive oil and place on the stove over high heat for a minute. During this time the "socarrat" or crispy bottom will form. Serve with a piece of lemon on the side and topped with a tablespoon of garlic aioli and a sprinkle of chives.

BOURBON STEAK

2800 PENNSYLVANIA AVENUE NW
WASHINGTON, DC 20007
(202) 944-2026
BOURBONSTEAKDC.COM
EXECUTIVE CHEF: ADAM SOBEL
HEAD BARTENDER: JAMIE MACBAIN

Chef Adam Sobel's flavorful salmon burger seamlessly brings together an array of components like his house-made kimchee, delicate ginger, and chili paste. Although each of these pieces is an essential part of the whole dish, it's the salmon's sourcing that the chef says makes or breaks the integrity of the final product. Whenever possible Sobel uses wild arctic char for the recipe, but points to trout as a great replacement if you can't find good salmon. What he does warn against using in this non-beef burger is farmed Atlantic salmon.

"Stay away from Atlantic farm-raised salmon," he says adding that much to the delight of many a chef, including himself, more customers are asking and are aware of the sourcing of all ingredients especially fish. "There are lots of nasty things associated with Atlantic farm-raised salmon. And, it doesn't taste good."

If you do go the trout route with this burger recipe, keep in mind that trout has less of a fat content than salmon, which you need to account for as you cook it. Sobel recommends cooking the trout to about a medium rare and notes that once you take it out it will carry over (or continue cooking) to a medium well. At Bourbon Steak, all the fabulous kimchee is made in house. At any given moment the chef always has a huge amount of it fermenting and goes through about a hundred pounds of cabbage a week. For those who don't have the time or space to do that at home, you can purchase some great premade kimchee at local Korean markets. But if you are on the fence about attempting to make the traditional fermented condiment at home, Sobel encourages you to go for it. He promises it's not that hard. Like so many other things in life, the most challenging part is waiting. "The longer it goes, the more depth of flavor," he says.

SALMON OR ARCTIC CHAR BURGER

MAKES 1 BURGER

For the ginger aioli:

1 tablespoon chopped shallot
6 tablespoons chopped ginger
1 tablespoon Dijon mustard
2 egg yolks
½ cup grape-seed oil
½ cup olive oil
2 ounces ginger, microplaned
½ lemon, juiced

For the kochujang sauce:

½ cup kochujang paste (sun-dried Korean chili paste)
1½ cups water
½ cup apple cider vinegar
1 cup sugar
1 tablespoon sesame seeds (toasted)
1 tablespoon sesame oil
1 lemon, juiced

For the burger:

4-ounce portion of salmon when in season
    (char is a suitable substitute)
Olive oil
Salt and pepper to taste
Ground espelette (a French chili pepper)
Kochujang sauce (recipe below)
Sesame-seed bun
Ginger aioli (recipe below)
Cilantro
Kimchee (found at your local Asian specialty store
    or made in house)
Red and green jalapeño (sliced very thin)
English cucumbers
Pickle spear

Special equipment: fish spatula and palette knife

To prepare the ginger aioli: Mix the shallots, chopped ginger, Dijon, and egg yolks in a blender and puree until it's a smooth, slightly aerated consistency. Slowly pour in the grape-seed oil, followed by the olive oil, to create an emulsion. Remove from blender and transfer to a large bowl. Once in bowl, mix all the ingredients together. Mix in the microplaned ginger. Fold the juice of half a lemon into the completed ginger aioli. The lemon juice helps brighten and bring out the flavors of the aioli.

To prepare the kochujang sauce: Combine all the ingredients in a bowl and mix.

To prepare the burgers: Lather the salmon filet on both sides with olive oil and season with salt, pepper, and espelette. Place the salmon on the baking sheet skin side up and place in the broiler for 2 minutes. Flip the fish over and cook for another 2 minutes. At this point your fish fillet should be at about medium rare. Brush on a light coating of the kochujang sauce and place back into the broiler and cook until medium with a slightly charred crust of the kochujang sauce.

Remove the fillet from the heat and let it rest for a minute while toasting the bun. Once the buns are perfectly toasted, spread a layer of the ginger aioli on both sides of the bun. On the top half of the bun, layer the toppings in the following order: cilantro, kimchee, jalapeño, and cucumber. Place the salmon fillet on the bottom half of the bun and place the top half of the bun with all the accompaniments on top of the salmon fillet. Garnish with a pickle spear.

THE JEFFERSON COCKTAIL

MAKES 1 COCKTAIL

2 ounces bourbon (like Bulleit)
¾ ounce Carpano Antica (an Italian sweet vermouth)
½ ounce crème de mûre (a blackberry liqueur, not blackberry brandy)
1 dash Old Fashioned Bitters (like Fee Bros)
Lemon zest

Combine all ingredients in a mixing glass and stir until well chilled (about 20 seconds). Strain into a chilled coupe or martini glass. Garnish with a wide swath of lemon zest.

BRASSERIE BECK

1101 K STREET NW
WASHINGTON, DC 20005
(202) 408-1717
BECKDC.COM
CHEF/OWNER: ROBERT WEIDERMEIR

When Brasserie Beck first opened, Chef Robert Weidermeir couldn't help but laugh just a little bit every time someone came up to him and remarked how he'd stumbled on something new. "There was nothing that novel about it," he says about the concept of a brasserie. "They are all over Europe. They are all over San Francisco. They are all over New York."

Where they were not all over was Washington, DC. And, that, was what made his venture a novel one—and still does. Before Weidermeir opened the doors to Brasserie Beck, you would be hard pressed to find a place inside the Beltway where you could order *moules* and *frites,* along with an international beer from a list a hundred bottles long.

When it comes to the mussels at Beck, and all the seafood he serves for that matter, Weidermeir goes to great lengths to ensure its quality and safety. The chef lists the origins of all the fruits of the sea he uses on his menus and even went down to Louisiana after the oil spill cleanup to see firsthand how the supply had rebounded. "I went down there with the USDA, the director of EPA, and representatives from the White House," he shares. "We went fishing. We ate the food. It all looked and tasted great."

For those who get a bit nervous about purchasing fresh seafood here at home, the chef first recommends finding a vendor who is very busy and moving product off the shelves. "It's just like a sushi restaurant," he tells. "You don't want to go to one that isn't packed."

Once you settle on a shop or fishmonger that make you feel comfortable, the chef says the best tools you can bring shopping are your senses. "The first thing I do with any seafood is smell it," he shares. "If it doesn't smell like the ocean or water, don't buy it. It's supposed to smell nice and sweet like the ocean. Then I look at it. If the eyes are cloudy it's not good."

PROVENÇAL MUSSELS WITH TOMATO, GARLIC, CAPERS & BASIL

SERVES 1

2 peeled, sliced shallots
2 tablespoons chopped garlic
1 tablespoon olive oil
1 pound, cleaned, scrubbed, de-bearded
    PEI mussels (leave in shell)
½ cup diced plum tomatoes
½ cup dry white wine or vermouth
2 tablespoons capers
1 teaspoon ground espelette pepper
2 tablespoons chopped small-leaf basil
1 whole garlic bulb
Fresh baguette
Fresh parsley for garnish

In a pot or heavy pan, sweat shallots and chopped garlic in olive oil. Add mussels, tomatoes, white wine, capers, pepper, and basil. Cover with lid and cook until mussels open up.

Take one whole bulb of garlic, wrap in foil and cook in 300°F oven until soft (about 30–40 minutes). Remove from oven, cut in half, and rub on slices of grilled or toasted baguette.

Cooked mussels can be eaten right from the pot or pan or transferred to a wide-rim soup bowl. Use baguette slices to soak up mussel broth. Top with chopped fresh parsley and serve with a good Chardonnay or Sauvignon Blanc.

CAKELOVE

1506 U Street NW
Washington, DC 20009
(202) 588-7100
CAKELOVE.COM
Owner: Warren Brown

Warren Brown knows how to keep a promise.

When he first started baking, Brown was frustrated by the need to find the right recipe in the right cookbook on the right page every single time he wanted to create something new. "I remember thinking I couldn't wait for the day when I didn't need to open a cookbook anymore, for the time when I could just recite a recipe off the top of my head," recalls the Cakelove founder and owner. "It was a little promise I made to myself that I would get to that point. The whole business really is a promise I made to myself."

Six shops and more than ten years later, the litigator-turned-baker has more than kept his word. Brown can rattle off recipes the way most people do their own phone number, and his story of leaving a promising legal career to pursue his buttercream dreams has landed him on *The Oprah Winfrey Show,* American Express commercials, and several other high-profile media gets. His sugar-and-flour empire sells slews of beloved cakes, cookies, and cupcakes each week and Cakelove now stands as something of a DC institution with multiple locations around town. All of his baked goods, like his Susie's a Pink Lady, are also known for using only natural ingredients for coloring instead of dyes or food coloring. In the case of Susie, it's raspberries—lots and lots of fresh raspberries—that create its pretty pink hue.

Brown first baked the cake for a friend's birthday party whose name was, wait for it . . . Susie. The original creation was a classic French genoise, but once he started making it at the bakery he quickly discovered that the American palate preferred a moister cake like the ones made from boxed mixes

so many grew up on. It's now a vanilla butter layer cake with raspberry buttercream. For those attempting Susie at home, Brown recommends always making sure there is buttercream on top and on bottom, sandwiching the berries. "Berries hitting the cake doesn't look good," he shares. He also suggests taking the time to line all the berries up so they are facing the same direction. "This is a beautiful cake to bake and serve. It's a fair amount of work and the labor of love shows with all of the colors and flavors that jump out with every slice," he says. "Fresh raspberries make a great statement, so pack the middle layers with them."

It is an eye toward this level of detail that clearly has helped him keep his sweet promise from a decade ago.

A word of help from Brown on the batter: "The cake is a relatively loose batter that will not look homogenous at the final mix. That's intentional. There is a fairly large amount of fat relative to the starch in the cake, which is necessary to balance the proteins from the all-purpose flour. The potato starch is a must; do not skip it or substitute cornstarch. Potato starch can be found easily in specialty baking aisles at your local grocer. The buttercream is not difficult to make, but requires the proper equipment. A candy thermometer and stand mixer are very helpful to have."

SUSIE'S A PINK LADY LAYER CAKE

MAKES 2 9" X 2" CAKE LAYERS, ENOUGH FOR A 4-LAYER CAKE

For Raspberry Puree:

12 ounces frozen raspberries
8 ounces granulated sugar

For Italian Meringue Buttercream:

5 egg whites
1¼ cups, divided super fine granulated sugar
¼ cup water
12 ounces unsalted butter
Up to ½ cup raspberry puree

6½ ounces (13 tablespoons) unsalted butter
    (room temperature)
14 ounces superfine granulated sugar
4 eggs

Dry ingredients (combine with a whisk and set aside):

8 ounces all-purpose flour
2 ounces cocoa powder
2 ounces potato starch
1½ teaspoons baking powder
1 teaspoon salt

Wet ingredients (combine and set aside):

1 cup half & half
2 tablespoons brandy
2 teaspoons vanilla extract

Special equipment: Candy thermometer, parchment paper

To prepare the puree: Combine the berries and sugar in a heavy bottom sauce pot and slowly bring to simmer.

Continue to cook the berries at a very low rate for another 15 minutes. They should not burn. Strain through a tamis or other metal sieve; discard the seeds. Combine all of the pulp that gathered on the strained side of the sieve with the raspberry juices. Set aside to cool.

To prepare the buttercream: Combine 1 cup sugar and ¼ cup water in a heavy bottom sauce pot. Bring to 250°F (Chef Brown recommends using a Taylor® candy thermometer).

Meanwhile, bring the egg whites to stiff peak in a stand mixer fitted with the wire whip. Begin slowly, but increase the speed to high speed when the sugar syrup reaches 210°F.

Slowly pour in the ¼ cup sugar when the whites are at stiff peak. When the syrup reaches 250°F, slowly pour it into the meringue in a thin steady stream. The mixer should still be running while the syrup is being added. Continue to whip the meringue.

Cut the butter into small pieces while the meringue cools. After about 3 minutes, reduce to medium speed. After another 3 minutes, add the butter. Add the raspberry puree and mix on low speed until fully combined.

To prepare the cake: Preheat oven to 325°F. Cream butter in a stand mixer on medium speed.

Change to low speed, add sugar, and mix for 3 minutes. Add eggs one at a time, turning off the mixer and scraping down the sides of the bowl after each egg is incorporated.

With the mixer on low speed, add the dry and wet ingredients alternately, starting and ending with dry.

Turn off the mixer and scrape down the sides of the bowl again.

Run the mixer on medium speed for 3–4 minutes to thoroughly combine all ingredients.

Line cake pans with parchment paper.

Fill each cake pan 2/3 of the way and level with an offset spatula.

Bake for 30–35 minutes or until golden brown across the top and a bamboo skewer poked into the center comes out clean.

Cool on a heat-resistant surface until room temperature. Use an offset spatula to release the cakes from the sides of the pans and invert onto a flat surface.

To assemble: Frost each layer of cake and stack atop one another.

CAPMAC FOOD TRUCK

Chef/General Manager: Brian Arnoff
Director of Operations: Victoria "Vicky" Harris
capmacdc.com
@CapMacDC

Brian Arnoff had a suspicion that if he built it they would come. What he didn't realize was that if he built it with wheels not only would they come but they would also line up for it. The "it," of course, is the ooey-gooey macaroni and cheese that he sells from his widely followed CapMac food truck. Arnoff, whose culinary journey took him to Florence, New York, and Boston before landing back in DC, always thought that someone should come up with a quick but high quality way to get a good bowl of pasta. Turns out he was that someone.

"I've always had this idea that I wanted to do a fast-food pasta concept," he says. "I always thought it was a shame that you couldn't get a good bowl of pasta quick. Then the whole food truck thing blew up and I thought the ideas fit together.

Clearly, Arnoff and his team—headed up by Chef Vicky Harris—have hit a comfort-food nerve. "On the grayest, darkest days, our lines are the longest," he tells.

Classic Mac

1 stick butter
½ cup flour
6 cups milk (warmed)
24 ounces white cheddar, shredded
    (preferably aged at least one year)
2 tablespoons Dijon mustard
1 tablespoon smoked paprika
½ cup roasted red peppers, pureed
Salt and pepper to taste
1 pound elbow macaroni

For the topping:

1 cup crushed Cheez-It crackers
1 cup shredded cheddar

Melt the butter in a large saucepan. Once completely melted, sprinkle in the flour and whisk to form a roux. Cook on high for about 2 minutes until the raw flour taste is just cooked out. Slowly pour warmed milk (you can warm the milk by pouring it in a measuring cup and microwaving it for 2–3 minutes) into the roux while whisking vigorously to avoid lumps. Cook the roux and milk mixture, or béchamel, for 3–5 minutes. Next add the shredded cheddar in two or three additions, slowly melting the cheese into the sauce. Finally, add the remaining ingredients: Dijon, paprika, red peppers, and salt and pepper to taste. The sauce should be thick and rich, with a bright orange color and a slight tang from the Dijon and red pepper puree.

Boil the elbows in salted water until al dente. Drain (but do not rinse), add to the cheese sauce, and cook 1–2 minutes more until the pasta and the sauce become one. Plate in deep bowls, sprinkling each with some shredded cheddar and a handful of crushed Cheez-It crackers.

Caucus Room & Social Reform Kitchen and Bar

Market Square North
401 9th Street NW
Washington, DC 20004
(202) 393-1300
SOCIALREFORMBAR.COM
THECAUCUSROOM.COM
Executive Chef: M. Brian Wolken

After more than a decade on Capitol Hill, the Caucus Room remains true to its original vision of bringing together people who want different things around the same dining room table. The steak house first opened at the beginning of the new millennium as a bipartisan venture of prominent Democrat Tom Boggs and former Mississippi governor and Republican National Committee Chairman Haley Barbour. Today the bipartisan restaurant also offers a second menu, from what it has dubbed the Social Reform Kitchen and Bar. The Social Reform offerings lean more toward small plates and lighter fare rather than the meat and potatoes of the Caucus Room menu.

"The idea behind the Social Reform Kitchen is the change of times," says Executive Chef M. Brian Wolken, a former photojournalist who is responsible for the offerings on both menus. "The reform is about what has happened to dining in DC over the last twenty years."

You don't have to sit in a separate section of the restaurant to order a Social Reform dish and everyone in your party does not have to commit to a food-coma lunch if one person wants a porterhouse. "It's not one of those places where you have to eat at the bar to get what you want," Wolken points out.

In addition to more small plate–style dishes, the Social Reform menu uses a lot of fish as a deliberate departure from the beef-centered vibe of the Caucus Room. Among the dishes are this one for Caramelized Sea Scallops, Chèvre, and Fines Herbes Risotto & Sauce Beurre Rouge. Choosing high-quality, dry-pack scallops makes or breaks the recipe, chef tells. "The dish really is all about the scallops," he says. "It plays off the flavor and texture of the scallop."

Caramelized Sea Scallops, Chèvre & Fines Herbes Risotto & Sauce Beurre Rouge

MAKES 6 ENTREE-SIZED PORTIONS

For the sauce beurre rouge:

2 cups dry, hearty red wine

½ cup red wine vinegar

2 thyme sprigs

2 shallots, sliced thin

2 peppercorns, black, whole

¼ cup heavy cream

1 pound unsalted butter, cut into 1-inch cubes

2 teaspoons kosher salt

1 tablespoon fresh lemon juice

6 dashes Tabasco

For the risotto:

2 tablespoons extra-virgin olive oil

1 medium yellow onion, diced small

2 cups Arborio rice

8 ounces dry white wine

2–3 quarts chicken broth, low sodium

2 tablespoons unsalted butter, room temperature

2 ounces Parmesan cheese, fresh, finely grated

4 ounces soft chèvre

½ cup heavy cream, whipped to soft peaks

1 tablespoon parsley leaves, finely chopped

1 tablespoon chervil, picked, finely chopped

1 tablespoon tarragon, picked, finely chopped

1 tablespoon chives, picked, finely chopped

1 tablespoon kosher salt

For the scallops:

18 sea scallops, U-10, dry pack (U-10 scallops are sold 10 or fewer to the pound and are typically the largest scallops sold. If you cannot find U-10 scallops then you can use the largest ones you can find.)

Salt, kosher, to taste

Black pepper, fresh cracked, to taste

1 tablespoon canola oil

1 tablespoon unsalted butter

To prepare the sauce: Add the wine, vinegar, thyme, shallots, and peppercorns to a medium-sized sauce pot over high heat. Reduce the liquid until it is almost completely evaporated. Lower the heat slightly and add the cream. Reduce until almost evaporated.

Using a small balloon whisk, slowly incorporate the butter cubes over high heat. Add the butter gradually over a period of several minutes, allowing the previous butter to become smooth before you add more. Once it is all incorporated, remove from the heat and immediately strain through a fine mesh sieve. Season with the salt, lemon juice, and Tabasco. Put aside until the rest of the dish is complete.

To prepare the risotto: In a small, heavy-bottom stockpot, heat the olive oil on medium-high heat until the pan begins to smoke. Add onions and sweat for 30 seconds. Add Arborio rice and mix until the rice is coated with the oil and onions. Once the rice is coated, toast the rice for 1 minute. Add the white wine to the toasted rice and stir constantly, until the wine is almost completely evaporated.

Working in stages, add enough chicken broth to just cover the rice. Reduce the heat to medium and slowly stir the rice until the stock evaporates. Keep adding the chicken broth like this until you have used all the stock, the rice is cooked, and the stock is mostly evaporated. The rice should be cooked but still have a "bite" to it—creamy and soft on the outside but the texture of the grain still intact. Remove the rice from the heat and set aside.

To prepare the scallops: Preheat a large, flat-bottom sauté pan on high heat for 2 minutes. Pat the scallops dry with paper towel. Season the scallops with kosher salt and fresh cracked black pepper. Add the oil in the pan and heat for 30 seconds. Place the scallops in the heated pan. Sear, on the high heat, until a golden brown crust forms on the top. Flip scallops and sear the second side.

When the scallops are almost done, put the pot of rice back on the stove on a medium heat. Slowly stir in the butter, Parmesan cheese, and chèvre, being careful to not let the rice cool too much.

Once the cheese is completely incorporated into the rice, fold in the cream and all the chopped herbs. Be careful to gently fold the cream in, as you would with a mousse.

Just before removing the scallops from the pan, toss the butter in and baste the scallops with the browned butter.

To serve: Remove the scallops and serve immediately atop the risotto and surround with the sauce.

Central Michel Richard

1001 Pennsylvania Avenue NW
Washington, DC 20004
(202) 626-0015
CENTRALMICHELRICHARD.COM
CHEF/OWNER: MICHEL RICHARD

Philly has the cheesesteak. Chicago has deep-dish pizza. Buffalo its wings. And, some have started to say, DC has the burger. Over the last decade or so the burger seems to have taken its place as this city's unofficial dish. This is in no small part due to the creative takes on the classic sandwich happening in the kitchens of renowned chefs like Michel Richard. Richard's lavish lobster burger, a perennial favorite among Central diners, often is held up as the gold standard of decadent burgers. The lobster offering, made of pure lobster meat, is one of several wildly popular non-beef burgers on the Central menu. The others include an ahi tuna burger, a chicken and lemon burger, and a lamb burger. But it's the lobster burger that owns the spotlight—to say nothing of the heftiest price tag.
The French-born Richard opened Central as a chic yet casual follow-up to his flagship Georgetown restaurant Michel Richard Citronelle. Despite the $30 lobster burger, the Penn Quarter restaurant is more affordable than Citronelle and the dishes,.a selection of American cuisine playfully infused with French flair, more approachable and familiar to most customers. (Think fried chicken, short ribs, and banana splits.) The burger menu is not the only place the chef re-imagines the norm. Richard's homemade version of the Kit Kat bar wows customers on a daily basis and joins the lobster burger as one of the restaurant's most talked about dishes.

LOBSTER BURGER

MAKES 4 BURGERS

For the tomatoes:

4 slices tomato, ½-inch thick
½ teaspoon granulated sugar
Fine sea salt and freshly ground black pepper
1 teaspoon extra-virgin olive oil
1 sprig fresh thyme leaves
1 garlic clove, peeled and thinly sliced

For the lobster burgers:

2 (2-pound) lobsters
Fine sea salt and freshly ground black pepper
¼ cup mayonnaise, plus extra for chip assembly
½ teaspoon grated fresh ginger
1 tablespoon (½ ounce) unsalted butter, preferably
    clarified butter
1 tablespoon plus 1 teaspoon olive oil
4 hamburger buns, homemade or store-bought
16 wafer-thin potato chips
1 cup mâche

Chef's note: The lobster is initially undercooked. It is placed in boiling water long enough to loosen the meat from the shell to make removing it easier. Then the lobster is cooked again after the burgers are formed.

To prepare the tomatoes: Preheat the oven to 225°F. Line a baking sheet with a Silpat or parchment paper. Place the tomato slices on the lined pan. Sprinkle with a light dusting of sugar, salt, and pepper, then drizzle lightly with olive oil. Top with the thyme leaves and garlic slices. Place in the oven for 30 minutes to 1 hour to dry slightly and concentrate the flavor.

Cool the tomatoes on the pan, then cover and refrigerate for up to a day. Bring to room temperature before using.

To prepare the lobster burgers: Place enough water to cover the lobsters in a large stockpot and bring to a boil. Fill one or two large bowls (to hold the lobsters) with ice water. Place the lobsters in the boiling water for 2 minutes. Remove the lobsters from the pot and place in the ice water until cold. Remove and drain thoroughly.

Working over a bowl, break the lobsters apart and reserve any juices.

To remove the meat, grasp the tail, twist, and pull to detach it from each lobster. Twist off the claws. Discard the bodies or reserve for stock or another use. Twist to separate the knuckles from the claws. Use kitchen shears to cut through the shell on the smooth side of the knuckles, and pull out the meat. Using scissors, cut down the center of the underside of each tail. Pull the shell back and remove the meat. Cut the tail meat lengthwise in half. Remove and discard the vein that runs along the top of the tail. Cut the tail meat and knuckle meat into ½- to ¾-inch pieces and place in a small bowl.

Pull down on the small claw pincers to loosen them and then pull them away from the claws. Crack the wide section of claw shell with the back of a chef's knife and pull apart to remove the meat. Cut the claw meat into 2-inch pieces, and place in the bowl of a small food processor. Blend on high speed to a paste. Season with salt and pepper, add to the chopped lobster meat, and combine with a rubber spatula.

Divide the lobster into 4 equal parts and form each into a burger just about the size of the buns. Place on a plate and cover with plastic wrap. Refrigerate for 2 to 3 hours to firm.

Combine the mayonnaise and grated ginger in a small bowl. Cover and refrigerate until ready to use.

Preheat the oven to 350°F. If you have a second oven, preheat the broiler.

In a large ovenproof nonstick skillet, melt the butter with 1 tablespoon of the olive oil over medium heat. Place the burger in the pan and cook on the first side for 1 to 2 minutes. Flip and cook on the second side for another 2 minutes. Flip again and cook for another minute. Transfer to the oven and bake for 4 minutes, or until warm in the center. To check, insert the tip of a small paring knife into the center of a patty, and then touch the knife tip. If it is warm, the burgers are ready.

To serve: Split buns in half, place on a baking sheet, and lightly toast under the broiler. Or, if you do not have two ovens, turn the broiler on once the burgers are removed, and toast the buns.

Spread about half of the ginger mayonnaise on the bun halves. Using the remaining mayonnaise as "glue," make four stacks of four potato chips each. In a small bowl, toss the mâche with the remaining teaspoon of oil.

Place the lobster burgers on the bottom halves of the buns. Top each with a slice of roasted tomato, a stack of layered chips, and about ¼ cup of mâche.

Co Co. Sala

929 F Street NW
Washington, DC 20004
(202) 347-4265
cocosala.com
Executive Chef/Pastry Chef: Santosh Tiptur

Santosh Tiptur didn't have his first taste of french toast until he was nineteen years old. And, if you pardon the cliché, it was love at first bite.

The Bangalore-born chef grew up eating traditional Indian breakfast foods and did not happen upon the classic American favorite until he started working in the kitchens of hotels in his hometown. "As an adult I fell in love with french toast," says Tiptur, who has played around with different variations of the dish throughout his career. The decedent French Toast S'mores he created for Co Co. Sala are both a personal and customer favorite.

Although the dish has many components, eleven to be exact when it's made at the restaurant, the chef reassures me that it's not a hard one to replicate at home. The milk chocolate mousse can be made up to a day in advance and, while Tiptur uses house-made marshmallows and cinnamon brioche, store-bought versions also can do the job. Be it store-bought or house-made, the chef does recommend brioche over other breads for his chocolate-and marshmallow-laden french toast. Brioche adds a texture and fluffiness to the end product and is easy to work with in this particular recipe. "Brioche is firmer when it's cold," explains Tiptur who worked as the executive pastry chef at the Ritz-Carlton, San Juan, and on cruise lines for twelve years before coming to Washington. "But when you warm it up it's as soft as cotton."

The Co Co. Sala chef traces his passion for working with food and putting flavors together back to India. As a young child he loved helping his mother cook and fondly remembers going to the market about twice a week to seek out the best vegetables and other ingredients for her. "I would take my bicycle and hang two bags off the handles and go shop for her," he tells. "I'd bargain to get the nicest vegetables for her."

Santosh Tiptur
Executive Chef
Pastry Chef

French Toast S'mores

SERVES 8

Milk chocolate mousse:

1¼ cups heavy cream

²/₃ cup egg yolk

²/₃ cup sugar

2 cups milk chocolate

1 cup heavy cream

1 teaspoon unflavored gelatin dissolved
   in ¼ cup cold water

2 tablespoons Kahlua

Banana foster:

²/₃ cup water

1 cup sugar

1 vanilla bean pods

1 cinnamon stick

²/₃ cup cream

¼ cup butter

²/₃ cup banana liquor

¼ cup rum

Chocolate ganache (for sauce):

½ cup chocolate, dark

²/₃ cup heavy cream

1 tablespoon glucose

1 tablespoon butter, unsalted

Vanilla-cinnamon sugar:

½ vanilla bean

½ cup refined sugar

¼ tsp cinnamon, ground

Egg batter for dipping the french toast:

1 cup milk

¼ cup heavy cream

¼ cup sugar

1 tablespoon vanilla extract

4 large eggs

½ vanilla bean pod

16 slices of cinnamon brioche or cinnamon bread

32 jet puffed marshmallows

8 dark chocolate truffle cut in quarters

16 graham cracker cookies

4 ripe bananas cut in ½-inch slices

To prepare the mousse: Start by whipping 1¼ cups of cream until soft peaks form.

Place the chocolate in a mixing bowl. Heat the additional 1 cup of cream and pour over the milk chocolate. Whisk together until well combined to create a ganache.

In a double boiler, whip the yolks and sugar until the sugar is slightly dissolved and then transfer contents to a another mixing bowl. Whip until the volume has tripled.

Add the yolks one at a time. Then fold in the ganache, the melted gelatin, the whipped cream, and finally the Kahlua, into the yolk mixture. Cover and refrigerate overnight.

To prepare the banana foster: Place the water, sugar, vanilla bean, and cinnamon stick in a heavy bottom pot and cook the sugar until it starts to turn a light amber color. When this happens the sugar will begin to cook quickly. Soon you will notice that the mixture will turn a dark amber color. When this happens that means it has reached caramel stage.

Remove it from the heat once you have determined that the mixture has reached the caramel stage. Add the cream and butter and whisk thoroughly.

Add the banana liquor and rum and mix well. Set aside.

To prepare the chocolate ganache: First place the chocolate in a medium bowl.

Heat the heavy cream and glucose in a pan over medium heat. Bring to a boil and pour over the chocolate. Let sit until it starts melting. Mix with a whisk until well combined. Set aside.

To prepare the cinnamon sugar: Cut the vanilla bean lengthwise. Scrape the pulp out from inside of the bean and mix it with sugar and ground cinnamon. Mix well and put it aside for later use.

To prepare the batter: Heat the milk, cream, and sugar over a low heat until the sugar crystals are dissolved. Add the vanilla extract and the eggs. Scrape the vanilla bean into mixture and mix well.

To assemble and serve the final dish: Slice the bread in ½-inch slices. Spread the chocolate ganache on one slice. Place 4 toasted marshmallows, one chocolate truffle cut in quarters, and one graham cracker cookie square on top.

Take another slice and spread the chocolate ganache and make a sandwich with the slice, which is topped with the toasted marshmallow, graham cracker cookie, and chocolate truffle.

Repeat this process with rest of the bread.

Dip the smores sandwiches you have just created into the french toast egg batter, making sure both the sides are not over soaked.

Heat a non-stick pan on the stove over a medium flame. Once a sandwich is coated with the batter, place it in the heated pan. Add a few drops of melted butter to the pan and cook until golden brown on each side.

Once all the bread is cooked, place the banana foster caramel in medium pan over a medium heat. Add in the bananas and toss until well coated. Transfer into a small serving dish.

Coat the french toast on all side with the cinnamon sugar mixture and then cut the french toast diagonally. Artfully arrange the slices on a large platter. Serve with the chocolate mousse and the banana foster on the side.

Comet Ping Pong

5037 Connecticut Avenue NW
Washington, DC 20008
(202) 364-0404
COMETPINGPONG.COM
Owner: James Alefantis

From the tabletops to the tomatoes, James Alefantis's touch is everywhere at Comet Ping Pong.

Each year Alefantis and his team head out to Shippensburg, Pennsylvania, for a pilgrimage of the sauce. First stop, the Toigo Orchard, a family-owned farm. There they help harvest the ten tons (yes, tons) of organic tomatoes the farm grows each year just for the restaurant. After a very long day of picking, the tomatoes are loaded onto a truck and then driven off to Punxsutawny, Pennsylvania, home of the clairvoyant groundhog and one of the area's last canneries where Comet makes all of its pizza sauce for the coming year. There, hundreds of pounds of tomatoes get peeled, stewed, seasoned, and stored, but not before Alefantis tastes and refines the batches coming through, making tweaks and adjustments along the way until the red sauce is perfect and ready to be jarred. Finally, the finished product gets loaded onto the truck for the journey home to Connecticut Avenue. Once there, the sauce is unpacked and stored below ground in the basement space that runs below the restaurant.

Alefantis's involvement with the final product at Comet does not end with the tomatoes. He also poured the cement for the pizza oven, designed the industrial-age-meets-slice space, and even hauled and refinished reclaimed wood to create the distressed benches attached to the table tennis–like tables in the dining room. Many a night he makes the from-scratch rustic pizzas that come from Comet's busy kitchen and he is responsible for dreaming up the concept of a neighborhood pizza parlor with table tennis in the back and indie bands late at night. It is this kind of personal touch that has allowed Comet to distinguish itself on the restaurant scene and it's his busy kitchen that has helped take DC out of the pizza dead zone. It's also what makes a true neighborhood gem, with kids and families and hipsters often eating alongside one another.

THE SMOKY PIZZA

MAKES 4–6 PIZZAS

For the pizza dough:

7–8 cups cups organic white flour
2½ cups water
½ ounce active yeast
Pinch of salt

For the red pie:

Comet Pizza Sauce made from Toigo tomatoes
    or seasoned pureed canned tomatoes
Mix of low-moisture mozzarella and fresh
    Blue Ridge Dairy mozzarella

For the smoky pie:

Garlic oil
Melted onions
Smoked and fresh mozzarella
Smoked bacon
Smoked mushrooms

TRANSFORMERS

In addition to helping to lift DC out of the pizza dead zone, James Alefantis can also count supporting new artists as one of his accomplishments. The former gallery owner serves as board president of Transformer, a nonprofit organization that supports and fosters emerging artists. Pieces from the talent supported by the artist-centered group can be seen around Comet, including the large scaffolding-like sculpture entitled *Suspended Landscapes* that dangles below the skylight in the pizza place's main dining room. Although the hulking piece by artist Mia Feuer looks like it weighs a ton, in reality it is made mostly of super-lightweight foam and is affixed to the ceiling with plastic ties.

Make the pizza dough: Place all ingredients in electric mixer. With the paddle, mix until the dough comes together (about 3 minutes). Then mix on a slower setting for an additional 7–8 minutes. Let dough stand at room temperature for 1 hour. Cut the dough into 4 or 6 pieces and shape into balls.

Place the dough balls in the refrigerator for an additional 3–4 hours. Be sure to take the dough out of refrigerator about 20 minutes prior to baking so it can cool down to room temperature before shaping.

To prepare the pizzas: If using a home oven, place the pizza stone in the oven and preheat on bake for at least 3 hours at your oven's highest listed temperature (usually 500°F).

Sprinkle a wooden pizza peel with semolina flour. If you don't have a pizza peel you can use a floured wooden cutting board or cookie sheet.

Hand-stretch the dough into something looking like a pizza (don't worry about it being exactly round).

Place on peel then ladle on some Comet Pizza Sauce and cheese mix, for the Red Pie. Or top with any delicious toppings.

Slide pizzas onto stone and cook 5–6 minutes, or until crust is puffy and charred in places and the cheese has fully melted. Use the peel (or a large spatula) to quickly slide under the pizza and remove it from the oven.

For the famous Smoky Pizza, top the dough in this order: Garlic oil, melted onions, low-moisture mozzarella, smoked mozzarella, smoked bacon, and smoked mushrooms.

Enjoy with a beer, right before or after playing PING PONG!

A FEW TRICKS OF THE TRADE FROM JAMES

"Garlic oil is a great thing to have on hand for many things and it keeps for a week or more (or freeze). The oil imparts the deliciousness of garlic while removing its bitterness or pungency. Simply submerge lots of sliced garlic in a good olive oil and very gently simmer until the garlic gets soft. Spoon oil and the soft garlic onto anything."

"Melted onions are also great to have around or freeze for onion pizzas or tarts or quick pasta sauces, etc. Simply slice many fresh white onions and cook in a large pan with lots of olive oil. Cook the onions VERY slowly and DO NOT brown. Add lots of fresh thyme while cooking and take the onions off the heat after they have released much of their juices and are soft."

"Buy a great smoked bacon (we use a brand called Old Smokehouse) and slice and bake it until it just starts to crisp."

"For the smoked mushrooms we slice up cremini (button) mushrooms and smoke them over our wood grill and then sauté with whole garlic cloves and olive oil. If you don't have a smoker they will be great just sautéed."

"We sometimes smoke our own mozzarella but a great local cheese is Blue Ridge Dairy smoked mozzarella."

DISTRICT COMMONS

2200 PENNSYLVANIA AVENUE NW
WASHINGTON, DC 20037
(202) 587-8277
DISTRICTCOMMONSDC.COM
CHEF/OWNER: JEFF TUNKS
EXECUTIVE CHEF: ALFREDO SOLIS

It sounds like a throwaway to say that something is so good you can put it on almost anything, but it's the honest truth when it comes to the Beer Mustard Butter at District Commons. The stuff truly holds its own on sandwiches, cornbread, veggies, meats, and breads, and I must admit that I have seen at least two people eat the stuff off a spoon at this Foggy Bottom restaurant, which sits right on Washington Circle. In house, Beer Mustard Butter comes served with a warm pretzel baguette that Chef Jeff Tunks sources from one of his favorite New York bakeries. The combination makes for a can't-take-just-one-bite experience and it pairs well with one of the many American beer offerings at the light-filled, modern-day, tavern-type eatery. If you want an earworm with your brew, order from the "99 Beers on the Wall" wall, but please keep the singing to yourself or you might wind up dining alone.

The greatest time commitment with this recipe comes from the need to refrigerate the mustard seeds, vinegar, and beer overnight, which means it's not something you can just whip up an hour before company comes over or during the pre-game show. But if you remember to do the first step the day before, the rest of the prep goes relatively quickly and is pretty straightforward. As with anything, the better the quality of the ingredients (especially when it comes to the butter, dark beer, honey, and mustard seeds), the better the final product. This recipe is intended for a large crowd, think Super Bowl party or family reunion, but leftovers freeze well.

Beer Mustard Butter

YIELDS 1 QUART

¼ cup black mustard seeds

¼ cup yellow mustard seeds

¾ cup malt vinegar

1⅓ cups dark beer

1 cup honey

¼ cup dark brown sugar

1 tablespoon salt

1 tablespoon allspice

1¼ teaspoons turmeric

½ cup dry mustard

3 cups butter, unsalted and softened

Combine the mustard seeds and vinegar with ¾ of the beer and refrigerate overnight. In a saucepan combine remaining beer with honey, brown sugar, salt, allspice, and turmeric and bring to a boil. Remove from heat and allow to cool completely. Once cool, transfer to blender. Add ground mustard and soaked mustard seeds with their liquids. Puree in blender until smooth.

Separate ½ cup of the mustard mixture and add to 3 cups of softened butter. Whip together until evenly mixed and season to taste with salt. Repeat with remaining mixture of mustard (combining 1 part mixture to 6 parts butter) or store in refrigerator for future use. Serve with pretzel baguette or other breads.

Equinox

818 Connecticut Avenue NW
Washington, DC 20006
(202) 331-8118
EQUINOXRESTAURANT.COM
Chef/Co-Owner: Todd C. Gray
Co-Owner: Ellen Kassoff Gray

Theirs is a romance of the food fairy-tale sort. Sous chef meets sales rep, sous chef and sales rep fall in love, sous chef and sales rep get married and open restaurants as they ride off into the sunset. OK, it might not be coming to a theater near you anytime soon, but it is more or less the story of how Equinox co-owners Ellen Kassoff Gray and Todd Gray met once upon a time. "I was a food sales rep and he was a sous chef," she tells. "He was trying to pick up his sales rep."

Fast-forward a bunch of years to 1995 and the pair, both of whom started working in restaurants as teenagers, opened Equinox, their first professional undertaking together. "We came up with the idea just by looking at what was around us naturally," Ellen recalls. "Food at that time had gotten so far away from seasonal and local focus. Now, of course, it's what's normal and expected."

Today the couple counts several other food ventures among their achievements, including the seafood-focused Todd Gray's Watershed in NoMA and the Sunday brunch program at Corcoran Gallery of Art. Once a month they roll out a full vegan brunch, a

concept close to their hearts. The couple embraces "domestic veganism" at home, which means they are omnivores outside of the house but cook without animal products of any kind at home. "The mission of the cafe is to have a balance of vegan, vegetarian, and traditional foods in a public space such as a gallery," says Ellen, who does the majority of the cooking at home. "The clientele really appreciates it. Whether you're a carnivore or full-fledged vegan, you should at least try to be plant-based one or two days a week. It's a great way to live and it's the ultimate in conservation."

Risotto Fritters

MAKES 36

For the fritters:

¼ cup olive oil

1 cup minced yellow onion

3 cups Arborio rice

1 cup white wine

6 cups vegetable broth

Water as needed

2 tablespoons butter

1 cup finely grated parmesan cheese

½ teaspoon salt

½ teaspoon pepper

Canola oil for frying

For the bread crumbs:

3 cups panko bread crumbs

2 cups flour

4 eggs beaten for wash

Heat a 4-quart saucepan on medium heat. Add oil and onions and cook for 3 minutes. Add Arborio rice and "toast" for 1 minute. Add white wine and reduce until dry. Add hot vegetable broth ⅓ cup at a time. Stir the rice and let it absorb the broth between additions. Cook rice for 14–16 minutes or until al dente. If broth runs out before rice is cooked, continue cooking with additions of water. Remove from heat and stir in butter, Parmesan, and season with salt and pepper. Pour risotto onto a sheet pan and cool in fridge. While the risotto is cooling, take the panko bread crumbs and run them through a food processor. This will help make for a smooth, crispy finish when the fritters are fried.

When the risotto is completely chilled, form walnut-sized balls using your hands. Take the risotto balls and one a time roll them in the flour, then the beaten egg, and finally in the bread crumbs that have been run through the processor. Repeat with each risotto ball and make sure to keep to this order—flour, egg, bread crumbs. Once completed, keep the fritters cold until you are ready to fry them.

Before serving, fry the risotto balls in canola oil until golden brown on all sides.

Estadio

1520 14th Street NW
Washington, DC 20005
(202) 319-1404
estadio-dc.com
Executive Chef: Haidar Karoum

Some people like to gaze for hours into the night sky. Others get their muse on by watching the waves break against the shoreline. For Chef Haidar Karoum, inspiration often appears from watching other chefs practice their craft. One of his favorite spots to spend a day in New York was a restaurant with a kitchen bar where he could observe other chefs carefully prepare each order as it came in. "I would go there and literally sit for hours and hours," says Karoum. "When it came time to open, we thought, why can't we do that here?"

Thankfully they did. The counter seating perched above a kitchen at the 14th Street tapas restaurant now also offers kitchen fans and casual observers seating where they too can observe the art of cooking as they order from the menu of small plates and cocktails. For a few weeks in the spring, ramps become a popular player on that open stage. A scallion-like vegetable often described as having the flavor of both garlic and onion, ramps play a key role in the chef's divine Ramps with Smoky Romesco & Manchego Cheese dish at Estadio, which not coincidentally is the Spanish word for stadium.

Karoum derived his inspiration for the dish from the Spanish wild onion *calçot,* another spring onion with a very short and anticipated season. In Spain celebrations called *calçotada* have grown up around the vegetable. The tender *calçots* are charred over an open flame and then dipped in romesco sauce. Estadio's version pays homage to this tradition and captures its smoky taste. When ramps, or *calçot* for that matter, are not available, leeks or scallions make for good substitutions. A glass of red wine with the dish, be it one using *calçots,* ramps, or scallions, is not mandatory but highly encouraged.

Ramps with Smoky Romesco & Manchego Cheese

SERVES 6–8

For the romesco sauce:

¼ white onion, peeled and cut in chunks

¼ whole jalapeño

1 medium red bell peppers, whole

1 tomatoes, whole

¼ cup olive oil, plus ¼ tablespoon for vegetables

¼ cup almonds, blanched and peeled

¼ cup toasted, cubed bread

1 clove garlic

¼ cup water

½ tablespoon sherry vinegar

1/8 teaspoon pimenton (smoked Spanish paprika)

½ teaspoon salt, or more to taste

1 bunch ramps or scallions, washed, rinsed,
 and roots trimmed
½ tablespoon olive oil
Salt and pepper to taste
¼ cup romesco sauce (recipe below)
¼ cup grated Manchego cheese

To prepare the romesco sauce: Set a grill or broiler to high. In a medium bowl, toss together the onions, jalapeño, red peppers, and tomatoes in ¼ cup oil and salt. Grill, turning occasionally, until they're charred and lightly sweating juice. If broiling, lay out vegetables on a foil-lined baking sheet.

Put all the grilled vegetables in a large bowl and cover with plastic wrap. Let cool for 10–15 minutes. Remove the seeds from the jalapeño and bell peppers and peel the peppers. Leave everything else whole.

While the vegetables are cooling, heat a pan over medium-low heat and add ¼ tablespoon of olive oil. Fry the blanched almonds, cubed bread, and garlic. Cook until golden, about 4 minutes. Remove the toasted ingredients from the oil. Save the oil.

Place the vegetables with their accumulated juices into a blender along with the toasted bread, almonds, garlic, and ¼ cup of water. Blend until combined, and then add the vinegar, pimenton, and ½ teaspoon salt. Blend again while slowly adding the saved olive oil. Taste and adjust seasoning. Set aside to cool to room temperature.

To finish: Heat a grill or broiler to high. Toss ramps with the olive oil, salt, and pepper. Grill about 1 minute per side, until lightly charred. Place ramps on a plate. Top with romesco sauce and Manchego cheese.

FIOLA

601 PENNSYLVANIA AVE NW
WASHINGTON, DC 20004
(202) 628-2888
FIOLADC.COM
CHEF/PARTNER: FABIO TRABOCCHI

Growing up in Italy Chef Fabio Trabocchi almost never set foot in a supermarket. Instead he spent Saturdays going from farm to farm with his father to get what they needed for the week. The best eggs came from one farm, the best chickens from another, the best tomatoes from yet another. After the best of everything was purchased, the cooking began. "I guess I am one of the last of my generation of chefs to have one foot in that past," Trabocchi says. "Even our water came from a natural source."

"When I woke up on Sunday mornings, there always was tomato sauce on the fire," recalls Trabocchi, the son of a third-generation farmer who had a passion for cooking. "Maybe there would be a duck roasting or my father would be carving a rabbit. Or maybe I'd be going down to a garden in front of our house to collect artichokes."

Vivid memories of taste, sight, and smell continue to guide him and the way he approaches his craft. At Fiola, Trabocchi almost exclusively stocks his kitchen from independent farmers. The chef's attitude toward experimenting with food he attributes to his Italian roots. "The first and most important thing to keep in mind is to keep it simple and don't overthink it," he says of this meatball recipe. "If you want a bit more ground pork, add it. If you want some more ground bacon, add that. If you want an extra handful of cheese, that's OK too. Trust me, this behavior is as Italian as could be. As long as the proportions are about the same it will turn out in the end. The Italians don't codify things. In Italy even the same thing with the same name is different from home to home, from community to community, from village to village. So don't be afraid to make the recipe your own."

Meatballs

3 garlic cloves, peeled
1 cup plus 3 tablespoons extra-virgin olive oil
3 cups white bread, cubed
3 cups heavy cream
1 pound ground beef
1 pound ground veal
½ pound ground pork
6 egg yolks
2 cups grated pecorino Romano cheese
6 tablespoons chopped Italian parsley
Salt and pepper
1 cup canola oil for sautéing the meatballs

Cook the garlic cloves over low heat in a small saucepan with 3 tablespoons of extra-virgin olive oil until soft and translucent. Set aside to cool down and mash the cloves with a back of a spoon. In a bowl, soak the bread in the cream until completely soaked. Leave time to allow the bread to fully absorb the cream. Place all the ingredients (except canola oil) in a bowl, including the garlic with oil and the soaked bread. Mix well and let it rest in the refrigerator for about 30 minutes.

Form the meat mixture into golf ball-sized balls. Heat canola oil in large sauté pan. Working in small batches, sauté the meatballs until golden brown on all sides and cooked through.

As rule of thumb, most ground meats will produce a good meatball.

FIREFLY

1310 New Hampshire Avenue NW
Washington, DC 20036
(202) 861-1310
FIREFLY-DC.COM
Executive Chef: Daniel Bortnick

Warm memories and nostalgia serve as the main ingredients for Chef Daniel "Danny" Bortnick's popular Chicken Matzoh Ball Soup. Memory, nostalgia, and a hint of dill, that is. So when Bortnick took over the kitchen at Firefly in 2007 with the mission to craft a menu around the idea of classic American comfort foods done anew, his mom's matzoh ball soup immediately came to mind. A traditional choice for a Jewish kitchen, but a rather unconventional one for a mainstream restaurant of Firefly's caliber. "You don't ever really walk into a good restaurant and see matzoh ball soup on the menu," explains Bortnick, who remembers eating the steamy soup at holiday meals and Friday-night family dinners when he was growing up in Rockville. "But I ultimately decided that I wanted to create a menu that had a connection to me."

Unlike his mom, who cooked her soup all day long, Danny advises only cooking the chicken soup—any chicken stock—for forty-five minutes after it comes to a boil, a tip he learned from a Chinese chef that he likes to pass on to others. "After forty-five minutes you've got all the flavor you are going to get," he says.

While the flavorful soup and the light and fluffy matzoh balls are a shout-out to his mom, the dill is a homage to the now-defunct Celebrity Delly, a suburban Maryland fixture when Bortnick was growing up where the matzoh balls were made with fresh chopped dill. Many of the Latino cooks who work at Firefly add chopped cilantro and avocado to the soup when they dine on it on the rare days when there are leftovers—something you can easily try at home when you are making Bortnick 's recipe.

CHICKEN MATZOH BALL SOUP

MAKES ABOUT 20 PORTIONS

For the soup:

4 organic chicken carcasses
4 cups chopped yellow onion
1 cup chopped celery
6 garlic cloves, peeled and cut in half
8 sprigs thyme
8 sprigs parsley
1 bay leaf
2 cups chopped carrots, placed in a cheesecloth bag
Salt and pepper to taste
4 quarts cold water

For the matzoh balls:

16 large organic eggs
1 cup reserved chicken fat, melted
1 cup seltzer water
2 tablespoons salt
1 tablespoon pepper
½ cup fresh dill, chopped
4 cups matzoh meal

Special equipment: A 2-ounce ice cream scoop to make the matzoh balls, although you can use your hands, too.

To prepare the soup: Place all the soup ingredients (chicken carcasses, onion, celery, garlic cloves, thyme, parsley, bay leaf, carrots, salt, pepper, and water) in a pot and bring to a boil. Reduce to a simmer and cook 45 minutes (but no more than that!). Skim fat off the top of the soup and reserve for matzoh balls. Strain broth through a sieve and adjust seasoning. Remove the carrots from the cheesecloth and pass through a food mill and then add them back to the soup.

To prepare the matzoh balls: Beat the eggs. Add chicken fat, seltzer water, salt, pepper, and the dill. Mix thoroughly. Add matzoh meal and mix well. Refrigerate for 1 hour. Bring a pot of salted water to a boil. With a 2-ounce ice cream scoop, form balls and drop into water. Simmer, covered, for 45 minutes and then shock in ice water. When cool, store the matzoh balls in Ziploc bags and date them for future reference. Matzoh balls can keep for about a week in the refrigerator and can also be frozen. Reheat the matzoh balls in the soup.

COLD HANDS, WARM SOUP

At Firefly, Chef Danny likes to use a small ice cream scoop to form his *knaidelach,* the Yiddish word for matzoh balls, which are a kind of Jewish soul-food dumpling typically served in chicken soup. But *bubbes,* and *zaydes* for that matter, across the land might say "feh" to that newfangled way and instead encourage you to get back to basics and use your hands. If you do decide to go the old-country route, keep a small bowl of ice water nearby and dip your fingers in it before fashioning each *knaidelach.* This tip, which will help keep your *knaidelach* light and fluffy, comes to me from the two best *knaidelach* makers I know, my husband, Jeff, and our dear friend Judy Finkelstein-Taff. I've never seen (or tasted) a bad batch from either of them.

FOUNDING FARMERS

1924 PENNSYLVANIA AVENUE NW
WASHINGTON, DC 20006
(202) 822-8783
WEAREFOUNDINGFARMERS.COM
FARMERS RESTAURANT GROUP CORPORATE CHEF: JOE GOETZE
EXECUTIVE PASTRY CHEF: COURTNEY GOLDIAN

Chef Joe Goetze remembers the moment he knew he wanted to be a chef. It was 1987. He was making $6.60 an hour working in the kitchen at the Hyatt Regency in Greenwich, Connecticut. Each morning, the space would fill up with the sounds of the staff talking about what they did last night, complaining about shifts or bickering over things that happened earlier in the week. It was crowded and noisy. Very noisy. That is, until the

chef walked in. At that moment the fighting and joking stopped. It got quiet. Very quiet. So quiet you could hear a silicon quarter teaspoon drop. "I want to be that guy," Goetze remembers thinking that morning. He was in high school at the time.

It took time and a lot of hard work, but now he is that guy. Today Goetze serves as corporate chef for Farmers Restaurant Group. He drives the menu and food decisions at the popular Founding Famers restaurants, built around the farm-to-table concept coupled with the American cooking tradition, and he works to keep the concept fresh and fluid. Still, the Culinary Institute of America graduate credits that first hotel job as an important layer of the foundation on which he has built his successful culinary career. At the hotel he did everything from banquet prep to coffee service to butchery, which was common practice at hotels at the time.

Founding Famers was also formed on a holistic approach, albeit a decidedly different one. The downtown restaurant, as well as its Potomac location, prides itself on sourcing natural and organic ingredients with a light carbon footprint whenever possible. It also is committed to passing along to customers the origins of the foods it uses in its kitchen. The fried green tomatoes and beignets are just two tasty examples of the dishes that come out of this approach. Goetze stresses the importance of keeping your oil clean during the frying process and notes that you can use the batter for the fried green tomatoes for just about anything. For the beignets he recommends adding a sprinkle of salt and filling them with ice cream or really anything sweet that you would put in a pie crust. However you decide to dress up the dishes, the chef encourages you to put your own spin on them. "Make the recipe once to get to know the recipe and then start to cook it to your own style," he says. "Then the recipe becomes your recipe."

FRIED GREEN TOMATOES

MAKES 4 SLICES

¼ cup yellow cornmeal

4 tablespoons panko bread crumbs

Vegetable oil for frying

1 large green tomato (or two small ones), cored and sliced into 4–5 thick slices

½ teaspoon coriander seed

1 teaspoon black pepper

¼ teaspoon garlic powder

¼ teaspoon onion powder

1 teaspoon kosher salt

¼ cup dry tempura mix

¼ cup prepared tempura batter (you will have some leftover)

¼ cup Founding Farmers green goddess dressing (see page 73)

¼ cup goat cheese, softened

Combine cornmeal and panko in a food processor and blend until fine. Set aside.

Add 1½ inches of vegetable frying oil to a large skillet and heat until very hot (preferably 350°F). Season the tomato slices on both sides with coriander, pepper, garlic powder, onion powder, and salt. Then bread tomatoes in the following order: dry tempura mix, prepared tempura batter, cornmeal/panko mix.

Place each breaded tomato slice very carefully into the hot oil (using a splatter screen will reduce the oil splatter). Fry until golden brown on one side. Flip and fry until the other side is golden brown. Remove from oil to a paper bag or to a paper towel–lined plate to drain. Portion the green goddess dressing and soft goat cheese into small bowls or ramekins. Shingle tomato slices on a plate and serve with the dips.

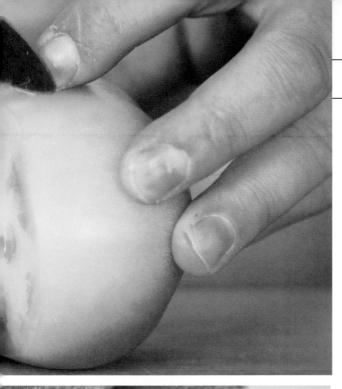

Green Goddess Dressing

MAKES 2 CUPS

½ cup finely chopped shallots

7 tablespoons extra-virgin olive oil

1 tablespoon minced garlic

4½ teaspoons white wine vinegar

2¼ teaspoons fresh lemon juice

2¼ teaspoons fresh lime juice

1 anchovy, diced fine

1 ripe avocado, skin and pit removed

½ cup mayonnaise

4 tablespoons fresh parsley, de-stemmed
    and chopped fine

3 tablespoons fresh tarragon, de-stemmed
    and chopped fine

1 tablespoon fresh cilantro, de-stemmed
    and chopped fine

2 tablespoons fresh basil, de-stemmed
    and chopped fine

¾ teaspoon fresh oregano, de-stemmed
    and chopped fine

1 teaspoon kosher salt

$1/8$ teaspoon black pepper

In a small skillet, sauté the shallots in 1 table-spoon of oil and set aside to cool. In a small mixing bowl, combine the garlic with the vinegar and lemon and lime juices and let macerate for 15 minutes. Add the anchovy and avocado.

Mash the avocado with a fork. Whisk in the mayonnaise and then slowly whisk in the remaining 6 tablespoons of olive oil. When the dressing is emulsified (thick like a dip), fold in the herbs, cooled shallots, and salt, and pepper to taste.

BEIGNETS

MAKES 20 1-OUNCE BEIGNETS

½ cup water
½ cup skim milk
½ cup unsalted butter
1 tablespoon granulated sugar
¼ teaspoon kosher salt
1¼ cups all-purpose flour
5 eggs
Vegetable oil for frying
Powdered sugar for sprinkling

Place water, milk, butter, sugar, and salt in a medium saucepan. Bring to a boil over medium-high heat, stirring occasionally. As soon as the mixture comes to a boil, add all the flour at once and mix vigorously with a wooden spoon. Continue to cook over medium heat until the batter forms a ball and pulls away from the sides of the pan. There should be a thin film that coats the bottom of the pan when the batter is ready.

Transfer the batter to a mixing bowl and mix on low speed for 30 seconds to release excess steam. Add eggs slowly, one at a time, allowing time between each addition for the eggs to incorporate. Scrape the sides of the bowl between additions. Once all of the eggs are incorporated, allow the batter to mix on low for 1 more minute. Place plastic wrap over batter, making sure it touches the surface of the batter, and let rest for at least 20 minutes.

Meanwhile, heat vegetable oil in a large, heavy pot or deep skillet (preferably to 325°F as this is the best temperature for the beignets). Using a 1 fluid ounce scoop (the size of about 2 tablespoons), drop balls of beignet batter into the hot oil. Allow to fry for 20 minutes, turning beignets over occasionally. Beignets are done when they are dark brown and crisp on the outside and cooked and airy on the inside. Drain on paper towels and toss with powdered sugar before serving. Serve warm with your favorite sweet dipping sauces (like chocolate, caramel, and raspberry).

Note: For both recipes, keep your batters cold and your oil clean.

Good Stuff Eatery

303 Pennsylvania Avenue SE
Washington, DC 20003
(202) 543-8222
GOODSTUFFEATERY.COM
Chef/Owner: Spike Mendelsohn

The Good Stuff Eatery, like all of Spike Mendelsohn's ventures, is a family affair. Mendelsohn's mom inspired him to create a spot where people could pop in and order really good handcrafted burgers, fries, and milk shakes. Both his mom and his dad came out of retirement from their restaurant careers in Canada to launch the Capitol Hill eatery with him, and the former *Top Chef* contestant's sister, whom he describes as his "partner in crime," found the location for the Capitol Hill shop and handles many other parts of the business. A host of cousins, aunts, uncles, and close friends round out the rest of the support team.

"One thing that has never changed for me is that this business, the restaurant business, is the epitome of family," the Good Stuff Eatery owner often says.

Mendelsohn moved to DC in 2008, in the height of election season, and he couldn't resist the chance to hold an election burger challenge pitting a McCain burger against an Obama burger. The Obama burger won the Good Eatery contest 4-to-1, and if you don't know how the real election turned out you must reside under a very large, very remotely located rock. In a hamburger-imitating-life moment, the forty-fourth president of the United States stopped by the restaurant in 2011 to grab some grub for a pre-birthday celebration before he hit the big Five-O. While President Obama did not order the applewood bacon, onion marmalade, and horseradish mayo–topped burger that bears his name, he did, by all reports, enjoy every bite of his Good Stuff meal.

This is Good Stuff.

Herein, where good people make good stuff, stands a restaurant committed to freshness, fellowship and friendliness significant to Washington DC and surrounding areas: GOOD STUFF EATERY. This, ladies and gentlemen, is more than a simple hamburger joint. It is a rallying cry. It is a whoop. A holler. A hail. And a salaam. Good Stuff is an aspirational articulation, an inspirational idiom and, quite frankly, the best way for the greater good of Washington DC and surrounding areas to enjoy handmade burgers, hand-cut fries and handspun ice cream that'll make you come back again and again and again. We hope you're hungry.

Prez Obama Burger

SERVES 6

For the horseradish mayonnaise:
   (Makes about 2½ Cups)

2 cups basic mayonnaise
4 ounces prepared horseradish
1 tablespoon cayenne
1½ teaspoons freshly ground black pepper
Sea salt

For the red onion marmalade:

2 red onions
1 cup Lucini Pinot Noir Italian wine vinegar
1 cup sugar

For the burgers:

30 ounces ground sirloin
6 potato buns, cut in half
Canola oil
1 pound applewood-smoked bacon
Sea salt
Freshly ground black pepper
1 pound crumbled blue cheese
Horseradish mayonnaise (recipe below)
Red onion marmalade (recipe below)

To prepare the horseradish mayonnaise: Add the basic mayonnaise, horseradish, cayenne, pepper, and salt to taste to a food processor or blender. Puree until smooth. The mayonnaise can be refrigerated in an airtight container for up to 1 week.

To prepare the red onion marmalade: Slice both red onions ½-inch thick. Add the vinegar and sugar to a pot over medium heat. Bring to a simmer. Once the sugar is completely dissolved, add the onions. Cook, stirring occasionally to prevent burning, until the onions are translucent and the liquid is reduced by half, about 5 minutes. Set aside to cool.

To prepare the patties: Roll six 5-ounce sirloin balls and form each ball into a patty. Arrange on a tray, cover, and refrigerate.

Toast the buns.

Heat a large skillet over medium-high heat and add just enough oil to cover the entire bottom of the pan. Line a plate with paper towels. When the oil begins to smoke, add the bacon and cook until crisp. Remove with a slotted spoon and drain on the paper towels. Drain the fat from the pan but do not wipe clean. Reduce the heat to medium and place the patties into the skillet. Season the patties with salt and pepper and cook for 3 minutes. Flip and cook on the other side for 1 minute more. Distribute the crumbled blue cheese equally among the patties and continue to cook 2 minutes more for medium-rare doneness. Cover with a lid for the last 30 seconds to melt the cheese.

To assemble the burgers: Place one patty on one bun bottom. Top the patty with some mayonnaise, marmalade, and bacon. Cover with the bun top. Repeat with the remaining patties.

Graffiato by Mike Isabella

707 6th Street NW
Washington, DC 20001
(202) 289-3600
graffiatodc.com
Chef/Owner: Mike Isabella

Chef Mike Isabella has been cooking Italian food—really good Italian food—for pretty much as long as he can remember. "I was rolling out meatballs when I was six," says Isabella, who as a boy in Newark, New Jersey, would spend hours on end in the kitchen with his grandmother. "I was a very hyper kid so they would keep me busy cutting up garlic, making pasta, cleaning dishes."

It was his grandmother who taught him the art of gnocchi-making, a careful skill that years later has resulted in one of the most ordered and loved dishes at his Penn Quarter Italian-inspired restaurant Graffiato. The family secret to really good gnocchi, Isabella tells, really boils down (pun intended) to two things—roasting the potatoes and avoiding the temptation to use a lot of flour. Flour makes the dish easier to handle as you are working it but in the end you get gnocchi that taste more like pasta than a potato dumpling. A lot of premade gnocchi err on the side of more flour than potato, which is why the chef encourages people to go ahead and try to make their own.

"Put in the minimum amount of flour as you can," says the former *Top Chef* contestant and *Top Chef All-Stars* runner-up. "I tell people to keep a little pot of water boiling and throw a gnocchi or two in when you are making them. If it floats in a minute or two you have enough flour. If it falls apart, you don't."

Crispy Potato Gnocchi
with Mushrooms & Stracciatella

SERVES 4–6

For the gnocchi:

4 large Idaho potatoes, washed

1½ cups all-purpose flour

2 large egg yolks, beaten

¼ cup zested Parmesan cheese (made on
a microplane to create very fine shavings)

1 teaspoon kosher salt

2 tablespoons extra-virgin olive oil

For the remaining dish:

2 tablespoons extra-virgin olive oil

½ pound shiitake mushrooms, stems removed
and cut into ¼-inch slices

½ teaspoon kosher salt

2 tablespoons unsalted butter

2 cups lightly packed fresh baby spinach

4 ounces stracciatella (can substitute burrata), found
at Italian markets or specialty cheese shops

1 tablespoon aged balsamic vinegar

Pinch of sea salt (preferably Maldon)

To prepare the gnocchi: Preheat the oven to
425°F. Prick each potato several times with a
fork and place on a baking sheet. Bake for 1
hour. Remove the potatoes from the oven and
let cool for 10–12 minutes or just until you can
handle them. Cut each potato open lengthwise
and scoop out the flesh. Pass the flesh through
a potato ricer into a mixing bowl. Stir in 1 cup
of the all-purpose flour, egg yolks, Parmesan
cheese, and salt. Using your hands, mix until all
ingredients are just combined, but make sure
not to overwork the dough or the gnocchi will
become tough.

Roll the mixture out into 12-inch by ¾-inch ropes.
Sprinkle with the remaining flour so they do not
stick. Cut into ¾-inch pieces.

Bring a large pot of heavily salted water to a boil.
Also set up a large bowl of ice water nearby.

In three or four batches, drop the gnocchi in the
water and cook until they all float, approximately
1–2 minutes. Using a skimmer or slotted spoon,
remove from the boiling water and shock in the
ice water.

Drain from the ice water and toss with the olive
oil. Cover and store in the refrigerator.

To prepare the remaining dish: In a large sauté
pan, heat the olive oil over medium-high heat.
Add mushrooms and toss to evenly coat, then
add the salt. (You may need to do this in two
batches, depending on size of pan.) Cook for
10–12 minutes or until crispy and cooked through,
stirring often. Remove mushrooms and set aside.

Add butter to the same pan over medium-high
heat. Once melted and slightly smoking, add
the chilled gnocchi and toss to coat. Let set for
1–2 minutes until golden, then toss to crisp the
other side.

Add the cooked mushrooms and spinach. Gently
toss just until spinach is wilted. Transfer to a
large serving dish or individual plates. Dollop with
stracciatella, drizzle with balsamic vinegar, and
finish with sea salt. Serve immediately.

KINGDOM COME COCKTAIL

MAKES 1 COCKTAIL

1½ ounces gin (like Bluecoat)
½ ounce Green Chartreuse
¼ ounce lemon juice
¼ ounce simple syrup
1 ounce passion-fruit juice (fresh, frozen, or
    use tangerine juice)
Brandied cherries

To create the cocktail, combine all the ingredients
in a shaker. Shake and strain into an ice-filled
rocks glass. Garnish with two brandied cherries.

Graffiato by Mike Isabella   8I

H STREET COUNTRY CLUB

1335 H STREET, NE
WASHINGTON, DC 20002
(202) 399-4722
THEHSTREETCOUNTRYCLUB.COM
EXECUTIVE CHEF: PABLO CARDOSO
CO-OWNER: RICARDO VERGARA

When you're having a Washington-takes-itself-too-seriously day, get thee to the H Street Country Club. Do not pass go. Do not collect $200 in campaign donations. And, for the love of politics, do not have one more where-do-you-work-who-do-you-know-inside-the-Beltway conversation. Instead go directly to the H Street Corridor to trade in that [inset the name of your very impressive employer] badge around your neck for a Skee-ball, mini-golf putter, and cold beer.

With its tongue-in-cheek moniker, The H Street Country Club is a no-vetting-process-required hangout that serves Mexican food and drink against the backdrop of boardwalk-style games. Upstairs is a DC-themed mini golf course that looks like Willy

Wonka and the Mad Hatter designed it on a dare. Actually, the course comes from the imagination and creative hands of local artist Lee Wheeler, who is responsible for the this-side-of-crazy-brilliant functional installation and all the other whimsy-with-an-edge art pieces throughout the multilevel bar. Favorite holes include King Kong scaling the Washington Monument, the zombie presidents (where Lincoln and several of his Oval Office successors join the ranks of the undead), and a poignant 3-D silhouette of the Iwo Jima Memorial fashioned out of more than a thousand plastic toy army men. Extra points for finding the tiny replicas of the Lincoln Theatre and Ben's Chili Bowl near the first putt and the face of infamous former DC mayor Marion Barry on the *Awakening* statue emerging from Astroturf near one of the last ones.

Unlike a PGA tournament, you can sip cocktails along the green. Tables are nearby, in addition to the ones downstairs and outside, where you can order off the menu that was crafted in conjunction with James Beard Award–winning chef Ann Cashion when the restaurant first opened. Local Chef Pablo Cardoso now heads up the kitchen at this fantastically fun spot that emerged during the first wave of development of the Atlas District. "This area has been so underserved for so long," says Co-Owner Ricardo Vergara. "Now new people are discovering it all the time. We feel very lucky to be here."

Dorado with Jalapeño Lime Sauce

SERVES 6

2 tablespoons finely diced red onions

3 jalapeños, seeded and finely diced*

2 sprigs of thyme

3 bay leaves

Juice of 15 limes

1½ cups white wine

1 pound asparagus

2 pounds fresh baby carrots

3 pounds of dorado (mahi-mahi), cut into
    8-ounce pieces

Salt and pepper to taste

4 tablespoons blended oil (vegetable/olive oil)

8 ounces (2 sticks) butter, plus 1 tablespoon to sauté fish

4 tablespoons heavy whipping cream

To prepare the sauce: Combine the red onions, jalapeños, thyme, bay leaves, lime juice, and white wine in a small pot and reduce on low heat until you are left with about ⅕ of the initial volume. Set aside.

To prepare the vegetables: Peel and remove the bottom end of the asparagus (about 2 inches) on a diagonal cut. Cut the asparagus into pieces about 2½ inches long and blanch by placing in a pot of boiling water for 3 minutes. Immediately remove them and place them in ice water (this will help keep the green color and will stop the cooking process).

For the carrots: Peel and then repeat the blanching process. Set the vegetables to the side.

To prepare the fish: Sprinkle the fish with salt and pepper to taste. Heat a medium-sized pan over medium-high heat and add the oil. When the oil is hot, place the fish in the pan and sauté until the bottom is golden brown. Flip the fish once and cook until both sides are golden brown (about 4 minutes per side, depending on thickness), set aside, and cook the remaining pieces the same way.

When your fish is cooked take the asparagus and carrots and lightly sauté them with a tablespoon of butter and a pinch of salt and pepper. Then bring your lime reduction back to a high flame and add the heavy whipping cream. When this mixture starts to boil, remove from the fire and add the butter little by little, mixing constantly with a whisk (do not stop whisking or your sauce will separate) until all of it is nicely incorporated into a silky sauce.

To assemble: Now that all the pieces for this puzzle are ready, put them together. Set the carrots and asparagus on the middle of the plate, place the piece of dorado right on top of them, and drizzle the lime and jalapeño sauce around that.

*For a spicier dish add more jalapeños.

HÄRTH

7920 Jones Branch Drive
McLean, Virginia 22102
(703) 847-5000
hiltonmclean.com/harth
Executive Chef: Thomas Elder

Chef Tom Elder likes to take to the open road. Atop his self-described Steve McQueen–style motorcycle, he rides through the Shenandoah Valley visiting the farmers and the land that helps stock his kitchen with fresh goods while at the same time soaking up hearty helpings of inspiration. For Elder, this kind of two-wheeled ritual is not about gimmicks or photo ops. It's just how he rolls, so to speak. It's also how he has built a menu with a true local soul at härth, his Tysons Corner restaurant.

"When we were getting started we said, let's put ourselves as part of the community," says the executive chef of härth, housed in the newly renovated Hilton McLean, of all places. "Virginia is such fertile ground. When we were getting started we thought we could actually build a real regional cuisine here."

Elder works with many cooperatives and regional producers to do this and even raises honeybees on one of the low roofs at the hotel. He got the idea to start beekeeping after a discussion he had with some colleagues about how there were no zucchini blossoms that year because there weren't enough honeybees around. "We wanted to do something to be part of the community," he tells.

Now he tends to four hives, some 160,000 bees, under the tutelage of his bee mentor. He moves the hives to make sure they get the right amount of sunlight, keeps tabs on the queen, and extracts honeycomb. The honey produced can be sampled in his signature bacon jam, and on the cheese and charcuterie trays. You can even stir some

into your tea. Furthering his commitment to the community, Elder also takes the bees on the road from time to time in a heavy-duty acrylic carrying case he designed for the purpose. "I go around to school to help educate children on healthy eating," he says. "I bring the bees so they can see that honey doesn't come from plastic squeeze bears."

Whether he is on the open road or out in the open in his kitchen, he couldn't be happier.

"It all came together when I came out here," he says. "This is the best time of my life. I don't think of it as work."

CRAB FONDUE

MAKES 2–4 SERVINGS

1 tablespoon onions, minced

1 clove roasted garlic, minced (see instructions below)

1 tablespoon butter

2 ounces fresh baby spinach, roughly chopped

½ cup heavy whipping cream

3 tablespoons grated Asiago cheese

1 tablespoon grated Parmesan cheese

1 tablespoon sour cream

1 teaspoon kosher salt

½ teaspoon black pepper

4 ounces Maryland lump crabmeat,
    freshly steamed

To prepare the fondue: Sauté the onions and roasted garlic in the butter. Add the spinach and lightly wilt.

Then add the cream and bring to a boil. Simmer for 10 minutes. Add both cheeses and stir until they are incorporated. Stir in the sour cream and season well with salt and pepper. Fold in the steamed crabmeat. Serve in a casserole dish on top of a base plate. Serve with rustic bread cut into chunks or cubes and arranged on the base plate.

Roasted garlic

½ cup vegetable oil

1 head of fresh garlic, whole cloves, skin peeled

½ teaspoon kosher salt

¼ teaspoon freshly ground black pepper

To prepare the roasted garlic: Heat the oil in small ovenproof saucepan over a medium heat.

Place the garlic in the oil and season with salt and pepper.

Place foil over top of pan and place into 300°F oven. Bake for 20 minutes.

Check garlic, it should be golden brown.

Remove the roasted garlic from oil with slotted spoon and place into a small ceramic plate. Let cool.

Use 1 clove or more (to taste) for the crab fondue recipe above.

Strain the oil into a small metal or ceramic container and allow it to cool. Once cooled you can store the oil in the refrigerator. The oil can be used for other recipes as can the extra garlic.

WHAT'S THE BUZZ

A Q &A with *Washington DC, Chef's Table* Photographer Emily Pearl Goodstein
about Capturing the Black and Yellow Beast on Film

Have you ever photographed bees or other stinging insects before?
This was my first foray into the field of insect photography. With the exception of the special gear, it is actually a very similar experience to photographing babies and toddlers—lots of running around and quick camera decisions.

Were you nervous?
Yes! About twenty-four hours before the shoot, I started to get nervous. My main concern was about a bee getting inside the bee suit. I brought a friend along so she could drive me to the emergency room in case anything bad happened. But once I got on the roof in my suit with my camera in hand, things were actually pretty peaceful (yet very hot).

What was it like to wear a bee suit?
The bee suit is perhaps the most unflattering item I have ever worn. It is also very hot inside there. There are lots of pockets and lots of elastic at the ankles and wrists. The whole getup looked even better when paired with the dish gloves I wore to protect my hands while I was manipulating my camera.

Can you really tell the difference between the bees?
At first glance, I couldn't tell the difference but once Chef Tom pointed out who was who I could really tell that the queen bee was a little larger than the others. She was also surrounded by the worker bees. The other interesting thing is that the honeycombs filled with honey are sort of white, not clear or yellowish as you'd expect. This was confusing at first because I wasn't sure if the bees had been very productive, but then Chef Tom explained where the honey was and where the honeycombs were empty.

Were any of the bees camera shy? Did the Queen hog the lens?
All the bees actually stayed away from the camera. I was expecting them to buzz around me and my gear, but as Chef Tom described it, his bees are very mellow.

Photo on right by Beth Kurtz

HULA GIRL TRUCK

HULAGIRLTRUCK.COM
@HULAGIRLTRUCK
CHEF/OWNER: MIKALA BRENNAN

Mikala Brennan knows better than to question the power of the Spam. The self-described Hula Girl food-truck chef, owner, truck driver, and dishwasher, can't really explain the fascination with the canned meat but sells a huge amount of it each week from her aloha-ed out surfboard-topped mobile Hawaiian restaurant.

Even with the two-per-customer limit, Hula Girl's spam musubi sells out just about each day that Brennan takes to the streets of DC with her truck filled with authentic Hawaiian food. Found almost everywhere in the islands from convenience stores to school cafeterias to the zoo, the rectangular snack basically is a fried piece of Spam over rice that is pressed together and wrapped with seaweed. "It's salty, it's savory, and it's oddly addictive," says the Oahu native Brennan. "It's one of those things you can go and grab at pretty much any 7-Eleven at home. It's portable. It's something that doesn't need to be refrigerated. It's even something of a rite of passage for newcomers who want to attain local status to eat a Spam musubi."

Hula Girl's offerings hardly are limited to the Hawaiian preserved-meat delicacy. She also serves teriyaki steak, chicken, and tofu that can be ordered over a salad in a *banh mi*–style sandwich or as a plate lunch island-style with two scoops of rice and a scoop of her fabulous macaroni salad. Brennan spent months and months perfecting her teriyaki to get it just right and up to her Hawaiian standards. The Kalua Pork also transports Hawaiians thousands of miles back home with its authentic flavors. Kalua, Brennan tells, is derived from two words in Hawaiian—*ka* meaning "the" and *lua* meaning "hole," which refers to the use of an underground oven or *imu*. Although she promises she does not dig holes on the Mall to cook her pork, she has mastered the art of re-creating the taste from five thousand miles away. She has done such a good job that Brennan counts the Hawaiian congressional delegation and staff members among her followers, along with many, many others with aloha in their hearts and on their minds.

SPICY WATER

You won't find hot sauce lined up with the condiments at the Hula Girl truck but a steady supply of Hawaiian Chili Water, ginger, garlic, salt and chili peppers blended with water and a splash of vinegar, will always be on hand to spice up any dish. "We don't really have hot sauce in Hawaii because we don't have a lot of vinegars there," Brennan explains. "But we use lots and lots of chili water. We have it out on the table where the Tabasco would go."

Kalua Pork

1 cup canola oil

½ cup Hawaiian salt (kosher salt can be used)

2 tablespoons all-natural liquid smoke (can be found in natural food stores)

2 fresh banana leaves (can be found in Asian markets)

10 pounds pork butt

Preheat the oven to 500°F.

Take ¼ cup of the oil and mix with the salt and liquid smoke to make a paste. Set aside.

Lay a piece of heavy-duty aluminum foil (approximately 18 x 18 inches) onto a work surface. Place one of the banana leaves onto the foil. Take your paste and spread half of this onto the banana leaves. Place pork onto the top of this, then use the remaining paste and rub the pork really well on the top. Use the other banana leaf on the top of the pork. Place another piece of foil on the top of the banana leaf. Then pull the bottom and top sheets of foil together to create a tight seal.

Place foil package into a large roasting pan, fill with 2 inches of water, then cover the pan with foil to seal in the steam.

Place the pork into the oven and drop the temperature down to 350 °F. Roast pork in oven until very tender when pierced with fork, about 5 hours.

Remove the pan from the oven and let cool slightly. Unwrap the foil carefully as there will be steam wanting to escape. Discard the banana leaves. Pull the pork out of the roasting pan—but reserve the juices! Shred the pork with two forks or with tongs. Add in some of the reserved juices.

Serve with some sticky rice and veggies for a great meal.

The pork can be refrigerated for up to 5 days.

SPAM MUSUBI

MAKES 10 MUSUBI

4 cups Calrose rice (sushi rice is a good substitute)

4 cups water

Sushi vinegar (recipe below)

1 tablespoon furikake (a seasoning mix of nori, sesame
    seeds, salt, and sugar easily found in Asian markets)

5 sheets of roasted nori or Korean laver

¼ cup soy sauce

1 teaspoon sugar

1 can Spam

For the sushi vinegar:

1 cup rice wine vinegar

½ cup sugar

1 tablespoon kosher salt

Place rice in a saucepan with water. Wash rice by stirring with your hand and replacing the water until it remains clear. Drain rice in colander, transfer to a heavy pot or rice cooker, and add 4 cups of water. Heat over medium-high heat and bring just to a boil. Reduce heat to low and simmer, covered, for 15 minutes. Turn off heat and leave pan covered for 15 additional minutes. Place the rice in a bowl and let it cool completely. Add 2 tablespoons of the sushi vinegar (see recipe) and the furikake to the rice and mix thoroughly with your hands.

Cut nori in half widthwise—this will give you 10 sheets. Mix soy sauce and sugar and hold.

Cut Spam into 10 rectangular slices about ¼-inch thick. In a large, ungreased frying pan over medium heat, fry slices until brown and slightly crispy. With the pan still hot, add the soy sauce and sugar mixture and slightly braise the Spam in the liquid. Put aside.

Using a musubi press, place a nori piece onto a cutting board. Position press on top of the nori so the length of the press is in the middle of the nori (widthwise). The press and the width of the nori should fit exactly the length of a slice of Spam. (*Note:* If you don't have a musubi press, you can use the empty Spam can by opening both sides, creating a musubi mold.)

Spread approximately ¼ cup cooked rice across the bottom of the musubi maker, on top of the nori. Press rice down with flat part of the press to compact the rice. Place a slice of Spam on top of the rice (it should cover most of the length of the musubi maker). Cover with an additional ¼ cup of rice. Remove the musubi from the press by pushing the whole stack down (with the flat part of the press) while lifting off the press. Fold one end of nori over the musubi and press lightly onto the rice.

Repeat with the other Spam slices.

Do not refrigerate musubi, as they will get dry and rubbery.

To prepare the sushi vinegar: Heat the rice wine vinegar in a small saucepan. Add the sugar and salt. Stir until dissolved. Let cool down and hold for use. You can refrigerate the sushi vinegar for up to 2 weeks in an airtight container.

THE INN AT LITTLE WASHINGTON

309 MIDDLE STREET
WASHINGTON, VA 22747
(540) 675-3800
THEINNATLITTLEWASHINGTON.COM
CHEF/PROPRIETOR: PATRICK O'CONNELL

Gregorian chants float through the air at The Inn at Little Washington's Windsor Castle–inspired kitchen as chefs clad in dalmatian-print pants move through the space with the grace and study typically reserved for prima ballerinas. Every item down to the smallest of measuring spoons has a purpose and place here, where calm is the objective and a dash of whimsy folded into large quantities of perfection is the secret ingredient. This level of precision and creativity is what has made a table at The Inn at Little Washington one of the area's—and the country's—most sought-after reservations.

"Happy people make happy food" stands as the mantra here at Chef Patrick O'Connell's kitchen, often described as being one of the most beautiful in the world.

Handpainted blue-and-white Portuguese tiles grace the walls along with a portrait of the chef and his beloved dogs, the same ones whose memory are honored with the black-and-white spots on the chef's uniforms. The strings of pearls worn by the female servers also serve as an homage to the chef's dogs, one of whom was named Pearl. As you might imagine, when both pampered pooches were alive, they ate well and even feasted on the first truffles of the season. One more example of how living and eating well is woven into the fabric of the restaurant.

"I've worked in a lot of 'hell's kitchens' and found them to be counterproductive environments that tend to short circuit the creative process," tells O'Connell. "We refer to The Inn at Little Washington as 'heaven's kitchen' and try to maintain a calm and relaxed work space. This helps reduce accidents, contributes to staff retention, and, we think, it makes the food taste better."

While the surroundings and spirit of the inn cannot be denied, the food is why legions of people make a pilgrimage to The Inn at Little Washington a must on their foodie bucket list. The menu is ever-changing, based on the bounty of the day and the imagination of those working in the kitchen. O'Connell's recipe for Lamb Carpaccio with Caesar Salad Ice Cream, which he shares here, is a decadent example of why so many mark the most special of special occasions at the restaurant.

FARMER IN RESIDENCE

JONEVE MURPHY, THE FARMER-IN-RESIDENCE
THEINNATLITTLEWASHINGTONFARMER.BLOGSPOT.COM

Before the sun comes up and casts its glow over the picturesque Inn at Little Washington, Joneve Murphy is up tending to the pretty gardens she grows on property. Hired by the Inn in 2011 as its first farmer-in-residence, Murphy grows much of the vegetables and fruits used in the kitchen of the world famous kitchen. Like everything else at the Inn, the produce she cultivates is far from ordinary. The majority of the expansive gardens and greenhouses on the property are filled with heirloom and unusual varieties like the tiny yet flavorful current tomatoes she grows that are so small that it takes about an hour to pick just one quart of them. Murphy, who studied environmental sciences and forestry in college, began farming at twenty-two, soon after graduation, when she was driving across country, ran out of money, and needed a job. That first job in the field launched her relationship with farming that ultimately landed her as the keeper of that which grows at The Inn at Little Washington. Murphy writes about the art of farming on her blog, The Garden of Eatin' at The Inn at Little Washington, http://theinnatlittlewashingtonfarmer.blogspot.com.

Carpaccio of Herb-Crusted Baby Lamb with Caesar Salad Ice Cream

SERVES 6

For the pesto:

2 cups packed fresh basil leaves

¼ cup pine nuts

¼ cup fresh parsley leaves

2 garlic cloves, roughly chopped

¹/₃ cup extra-virgin olive oil

½ cup freshly grated Parmesan cheese, preferably grated on a microplane

½ teaspoon freshly squeezed lemon juice

Sugar, salt, and freshly ground pepper to taste

For the croutons:

2 cups vegetable or grape-seed oil

1 whole garlic clove, peeled

1 sprig fresh rosemary

6–8 slices of baguette or French bread, cut into 1-inch cubes (approximately 2 cups)

Salt to taste

For the lamb carpaccio:

1–1½ pounds of lamb loin, off the bone and trimmed of all sinew and fat

½ cup dried oregano

½ cup dried thyme

½ cup dried basil

½ cup dried tarragon

Grape-seed or vegetable oil for searing

For the Caesar dressing:

1 large egg yolk

6 tablespoons red wine vinegar

1 tablespoon fresh lemon juice

2 teaspoons Dijon mustard

1½ teaspoons Worcestershire sauce

¼ cup grated Parmesan cheese

1 large garlic clove, minced

1 anchovy fillet, minced

Pinch of cayenne

¹/₃ cup extra-virgin olive oil

¼ cup salad or vegetable oil

Salt and freshly ground pepper to taste

For the Caesar salad ice cream:

7 large egg yolks

¹/₃ cup sugar

4¹/₃ cups whole milk

¾ cup powdered milk

1¹/₃ cups freshly grated Parmesan cheese

4 anchovy fillets, minced

2 tablespoons minced garlic

1 tablespoon Worcestershire sauce

2 tablespoons Dijon mustard

Salt and pepper to taste

3 red pearl onions, peeled and sliced in paper-thin rings

1 tablespoon capers

2 tablespoons finely chopped chives

½ cup baby arugula leaves, washed

6 leaves from a heart of romaine lettuce

½ cup grated Parmesan cheese

To prepare the pesto: In a blender or food processor combine the basil, pine nuts, parsley, and garlic. Puree until smooth. With the motor running add the olive oil in a thin stream.

Add the Parmesan and then season to taste with the lemon juice, sugar, salt, and pepper. Keep refrigerated until ready to use.

To prepare the croutons: In a heavy, 1-quart saucepan over medium-high heat, heat the oil to about 350°F. Add the garlic clove to season the oil. Once the clove is golden brown but not burned, remove from the oil and discard. Add the sprig of rosemary and fry for 30 seconds or so, then remove and discard.

Add the croutons in two batches and fry until golden brown. Remove the croutons from the oil with a slotted spoon or spider and drain on paper towels. Season with salt. Set aside until ready to use.

To prepare the lamb carpaccio: Season the lamb loin with salt and pepper and allow it to rest at room temperature for 15 minutes.

In a small bowl combine the herbs. Coat the loin with the mixture.

In a heavy-bottom or cast-iron skillet over medium-high heat, add the grape-seed oil until it is about 1/8–1/4 inch deep. Once hot, add the loin and evenly sear the lamb on all sides.

Remove from the pan and allow to cool, preferably on a rack. Once cooled, wrap in plastic wrap and freeze until ready to use. (Freezing allows you to get paper-thin slices.)

To prepare the dressing: Combine the yolk, vinegar, lemon juice, mustard, Worcestershire, Parmesan, garlic, anchovies, and cayenne in a food processor or blender. With the motor running, add the oils in a thin stream. Season with salt and pepper. Reserve in the refrigerator until ready to use. The dressing will keep up to 4 days.

To prepare the Caesar salad ice cream: In a large bowl, whisk together the yolks and sugar. In a large saucepan over medium heat combine the milk, powdered milk, Parmesan cheese, anchovies, and garlic and bring just to a boil, stirring constantly.

Place the egg yolk mixture in the top of a double boiler and slowly whisk in the hot milk mixture. Set the mixture over a pot of simmering water and whisk until the mixture thickens enough to coat the back of a spoon.

Remove the mixture from heat and let cool. Whisk in Worcestershire, Dijon, and season with salt and pepper to taste.

Freeze in an ice cream maker according to the manufacturer's instructions. The ice cream can keep in the freezer for up to a month or until ready to serve.

To assemble: Spread 1 tablespoon of pesto in an arc across the corner of the plate.

Scoop the Caesar ice cream into small balls and keep in the freezer until ready to serve.

Remove the lamb from the freezer and cut into paper-thin slices. Arrange the slices into four or five overlapping rows in the center of six chilled serving plates.

Sprinkle the lamb with the red onion slices, capers, chives, croutons, and arugula.

In a medium bowl, toss the lettuce leaves with enough of the Caesar dressing to thoroughly coat and place the leaves on the corner opposite the pesto. Sprinkle generously with Parmesan cheese.

Scatter 3–4 small scoops of Caesar ice cream across the lamb and serve immediately.

J&G Steakhouse

515 15th Street, NW
Washington, DC 20004
(202) 661-2440
JGSTEAKHOUSEDC.COM
Chef/Owner: Jean-Georges Vongerichten
Executive Chef: Philippe Reininger

It's near impossible to forget that you are in the nation's capital when you step into the elegant yet modern J&G Steakhouse. The graceful dining room's sweeping windows hold views of the city's most recognizable landmarks, looking out onto iconic sites like the Washington Monument and the White House, the restaurant's high-profile neighbor. The grandeur of the impressive space is reflected in the food, service, atmosphere, and, very often, the clientele who dine there.

Famed restaurateur and chef Jean-Georges Vongerichten tapped Chef Philippe Reininger to oversee the kitchen when he opened J&G in 2009. Reininger grew up in France, steeped in the country's culinary tradition. "Food definitely was a very important part of each day," says Reininger. "It was important to us to meet at the table and share what happened during our day."

Giving people a table to meet at and putting good food on it would become Reininger's professional path. One summer when he was a student, a friend of Reininger's family who owned a restaurant offered him a job helping out around the cafe. Reininger was immediately attracted to the business of restaurants and from there he went on to pursue his formal training and work at some of the finest restaurants in Europe and the United States. His path led him to meet Jean-Georges Vongerichten, who became Reininger's mentor and ultimately brought the chef to Washington, DC, to help open the upscale steak house housed in the W Hotel Washington, DC.

The J&G lamb chop and spinach speak to what the pair has brought to the menu. Both are versions of classic steak-house dishes done with a hint of newness, like the decision to add fresh basil to what often is just a standard creamed spinach side dish.

GRILLED LAMB CHOPS WITH
MUSHROOM BOLOGNESE & PECORINO

SERVES 4

For the lamb:

12 lamb chops
Salt
Freshly ground black pepper
Thyme leaves from 4 or 5 sprigs
Extra-virgin olive oil

For the bolognese:

1 tablespooons extra-virgin olive oil
1 garlic clove, peeled and minced
2 tablespoons finely diced Spanish onions
Pinch of salt
1½ teaspoons fennel, finely diced
Pinch of ground fennel seed
12 ounces grape-seed oil
3 ounces cremini mushrooms, cleaned and stem
    trimmed, sliced thinly
1 ounce shiitake mushrooms, cleaned and stem
    removed, sliced thinly
4 ounces cremini mushrooms, cleaned and stem
    trimmed, diced very small
1½ ounce shiitake mushrooms, cleaned and stem
    removed, diced very small
⅓ cup crushed San Marzano canned plum tomatoes
½ cup water
Pinch of oregano

For the chili oil:

1 teaspoon annato seeds
½ teaspoon hot smoked paprika
¼ teaspoon ground fennel seeds
¼ cup grapeseed oil

1 bunch broccoli rabe
1 tablespoon olive oil
Pinch of salt
1 teaspoon chili flakes
Chili oil
¼ cup pecorino, microplaned

To prepare the lamb: Season lamb chops with salt and pepper and press thyme leaves into meat. Drizzle with oil and grill until done.

To prepare the bolognese: Heat the oil in a nonstick pan over medium heat. Add the garlic and cook until light golden brown. Add the onions and the salt and turn the heat down to low. Cook until well caramelized, then add the fennel and fennel seed and continue to cook until the fennel has softened. Remove from heat and reserve.

Put oil in a deep, heavy pot and heat until almost smoking. Add sliced mushrooms and fry until deeply caramelized. Drain, shaking out excess oil, and set aside. Return oil to the pot and repeat process with diced mushrooms.

Combine tomatoes and water with mushrooms in a pot and cook over medium heat until thick and almost dry. Season to taste with salt and oregano.

To prepare the chili oil: Combine annato, paprika, fennel seed, and oil in a small pan and bring to a low simmer. Turn off heat, cover, and let cool to room temp. Strain.

Blanch and shock the broccoli rabe. Reheat in a sauté pan with olive oil, salt, and chili flakes. Arrange broccoli rabe in the center of a hot plate and place lamb on top. Top each chop with a generous mound of mushroom Bolognese and top with a generous flurry of microplaned pecorino. Drizzle with chili oil.

CREAMED SPINACH WITH BASIL

SERVES 4

For the cream:

1½ cups heavy cream
1½ teaspoons cornstarch
1½ teaspoons salt
Pinch of finely ground white pepper
Pinch of finely ground nutmeg

1 pound fresh mature spinach
2 ounces fresh basil
1 cup cream reduction

To prepare the cream: Whisk a little cream into the cornstarch to make a slurry, then whisk slurry into remaining cream. In a large pot with a wide surface area, bring mixture to a simmer and reduce until it measures 1 cup. Season to taste with the salt, pepper, and nutmeg.

In a large pot of boiling, salted water, submerge the spinach for about 30 seconds, or until bright green. Remove spinach with a slotted spoon and drain, then immediately plunge spinach into a bowl of ice water to stop the cooking. Remove and squeeze out all excess moisture.

Repeat with basil leaves.

To assemble: Combine spinach, basil, and cream reduction in a saucepan and heat until spinach is hot and glazed.

Jaleo DC

480 7th Street NW
Washington, DC 20004
(202) 628-7949
jaleo.com
Chef/Owner: José Andrés
Head Chef: Ramon Martinez

Choosing a table at the downtown Jaleo almost is as fun as choosing what to eat.

If you feel like playing with your food, head to one of the custom-designed working foosball tables near the front of the restaurant, complete with artist-made figurines—one set is men vs. women and the other is traditional Spanish dolls, like a flamenco dancer and bullfighters. The stools surrounding the tables are created from Vespa scooter seats. If you have romance on the mind, reserve one of the love tables tucked away behind floor-to-ceiling metal curtains for extra privacy. And, for days when you are feeling chatty and outgoing, head to one of the communal tables surrounded by an assortment of different chairs, including one crafted from recycled plastic.

"Everything here has a story," says the delightful Chef Ramon Martinez as he moves through the newly designed space pointing to other highlights like the hanging lights created from books, oversized original murals of people on the go, and a masked bull head that he jokes he should wire to growl when guests sit down.

The food here also tells a story of José Andrés's vision of a tapas restaurant that reflects the rich regional diversity of classical and contemporary Spanish cuisine. Martinez continues that vision as head chef, putting spins on dishes like these two that speak to his own personal relationship with Spanish cooking as well as the broader tradition of Spanish tapas. Martinez stresses the importance of using good quality extra-virgin olive oil when you make these recipes at home and premium Spanish anchovies. He adds that many Americans that think they don't like anchovies change their minds after they finally try the Spanish ones. "It's like they are tasting them for the first time," Martinez says.

Escalibada Catalana con Anchoas

CATALAN ROASTED VEGETABLES WITH ANCHOVIES

SERVES 6

Roasted vegetables:

1 large eggplant
2 red bell peppers
2 tablespoons Spanish extra-virgin olive oil
Kosher salt to taste
1 large Vidalia onion, peeled and cut into 1-inch slices

Escalibada dressing:

1 cup roasted vegetable juice (reserved from
    roasted vegetables)
1½ cups Spanish extra-virgin olive oil
½ cup Spanish sherry vinegar
Kosher salt to taste

9 premium quality Spanish anchovy fillets
Sea salt to taste
2 tablespoons chopped parsley

To prepare the vegetables: Coat the eggplant and red pepper with the olive oil and sprinkle with salt. Cook on a grill over medium heat, making sure to turn the vegetables and cook evenly. Keep on the grill for about 30 minutes or until fully cooked.

Place the eggplant in one container and the red peppers in a separate container. Cover both containers with plastic and set aside for 20 minutes to steam.

Peel the eggplant and discard the skin. Cut the eggplant flesh into 1-inch wide strips and discard the seeds. Save the juice for later use.

Peel the red peppers and cut in 1-inch thick strips and set aside. Reserve the juice as well. Coat the onion with olive oil and salt. Roast in the oven for 20 minutes at 350° F. Once they are cooked and brown let cool and set aside until needed.

To prepare the dressing: In a small pot, reduce the roasted vegetable juice by half and set aside. In a bowl, combine the vegetable juice reduction, olive oil, and vinegar then whisk. Adjust salt to taste and save for later use.

To serve: On a plate, place the roasted eggplant and pepper slices. Top with the roasted onions and the anchovy fillets. Generously dress with the escalibada dressing. Season with salt, garnish with the herbs, and serve.

Gambas al Ajillo

Sautéed Shrimp with Garlic and Guindilla Pepper

SERVES 5

Sautéed shrimp:

4 cloves of garlic, peeled
¼ cup Spanish extra-virgin Olive Oil
5 Arbol chilis
1 pound Shrimp White 31/35 peeled and deveined,
    or your preferred size
5 tablespoons of brandy
5 tablespoons lemon Juice
½ cup brava sauce (recipe below)
Kosher salt to taste

Brava sauce:

2 tablespoons vegetable oil
1 ounce whole garlic, peeled and sliced
2 Arbol chili
2 tablespoons sugar
2 tablespoons Spanish sherry vinegar
1 tablespoon tomato paste
2 pounds whole canned tomatoes (pureed)
1 tablespoon Spanish sweet pimenton
Kosher salt to taste

2 tablespoons chopped parsley

To prepare the shrimp: Thinly slice the garlic cloves with a knife, mandoline, or slicer and set aside. In a large skillet, heat the oil over medium heat. Add the garlic and cook until it begins to fry. Add the Arbol chili and cook for 1 minute. Turn the heat up to high and add the shrimp. When the shrimp starts to change color, add the brandy, lemon juice, and brava sauce then stir to combine. Remove from the heat, season with salt and serve.

To prepare the sauce: In a medium size pot over medium heat, add the oil, garlic, and Arbol chili, and sauté slowly until they start to brown. Add the sugar and stir until it melts. Add the vinegar and tomato paste and cook for a few minutes. Pour in the tomato puree and simmer until almost dry. Add the pimenton and adjust seasoning with salt if necessary. Strain through a sieve and reserve for later use.

To serve: Stack the shrimp into 5 shallow bowls, garnish with the parsley and serve.

Kaz Sushi Bistro

1915 Eye Street NW
Washington, DC 20006
(202) 530-5500
KAZSUSHIBISTRO.COM
Chef/Owner: Kazuhiro "Kaz" Okochi

Chef Kazuhiro "Kaz" Okochi's childhood memories of Nagoya, Japan, are dotted with recollections of cooking. In third grade he decided to surprise his mom by making her dinner on her birthday. The young boy made fried rice and flan from recipes he found on the back of the monthly school lunch menu. (She, of course, cried lots of happy mom tears.) In the fifth grade the future owner of a bistro bearing his name remembers attempting to bake cakes in his family's kitchen from recipes in his mother's cookbooks. (He didn't have the right electric mixer so they turned out kind of flat.) And, a few years later, even as sports and schoolwork took up most of his time, he remembers being obsessed with a television show called *Cooking Heaven,* where the head of a culinary school prepared different dishes for viewers at home.

"He was my idol," Okochi tells. "I later would go to his culinary school."

The inspiration for the Sea Trout Napoleon, something of a signature dish of his, is also a product of his memory. After he graduated from the esteemed Tsuji Culinary Institute in Osaka, Okochi got a job at a sushi restaurant. His owner took the team out

a few times a year on holidays. On one particular occasion the group went out to a restaurant in Kobe's Chinatown, where they dined on a whole Thai snapper with sliced peanuts and cilantro. All these years later the dish still leaves an impression. "I still remembered the dish," he says. "I created this one based on my memory of it."

Fresh, high-quality fish stands as the key to creating Okochi 's homage to that Kobe meal long ago. If you can't find good trout he recommends substituting sea bass or a white-meat fish like flounder. The marinade can be prepared ahead but tossing the fish in the sauce and final assembly need to be done just before serving.

SEA TROUT NAPOLEON

SERVES 4

For the marinade:

1 tablespoon rice vinegar
3 tablespoons soy sauce
1 teaspoon sugar
1 tablespoon sesame oil
1 teaspoon chili sesame oil
¼ teaspoon chile powder
¼ teaspoon ginger juice

For the fried wontons:

Vegetable oil as needed for frying
8 wonton skins, cut into 2½-inch rounds

For the beet dressing:

2 tablespoons white balsamic vinegar
2 tablespoons rice vinegar
¼ cup canola oil
½ teaspoon sugar
1 tablespoon beet juice

For the sea trout:

1 (8-ounce) sea trout fillet, skinned and finely diced
2 tablespoons coarsely chopped unsalted peanuts
2 sprigs cilantro, stemmed and minced

For the garnish:

Assorted red and green seaweed

To prepare the marinade: In a small bowl, combine all the ingredients and reserve.

To prepare the fried wontons: In a medium saucepan, heat about a ½-inch of oil to 400°F. Add the wonton skins, fry until golden brown and crisp, and remove to a paper towel–lined half sheet pan to drain and cool.

To prepare the beet dressing: In a small bowl, combine all the ingredients, whisking to incorporate, and set aside.

To prepare the sea trout: In a medium bowl, combine all of the ingredients including the marinade, tossing to incorporate right before serving.

To assemble the napoleon: Place half of the fried wontons on a flat work surface and spoon half of the sea trout on top. Place the remaining fried wontons on top, finishing with the remaining trout. Place a sea trout napoleon in the center of a plate, garnish with seaweed, and drizzle beet dressing.

Serve immediately.

THE LIBERTY TREE

1016 H STREET NE
WASHINGTON, DC 20002
(202) 396-8733
LIBERTYTREEDC.COM
OWNER: SCOTT HAMILTON
CHEF: GRAIG GLUFLING

Scott Hamilton came down to DC after college for what he thought would be a short stint tending bar, and he never stopped. The New England native wound up opening Hamilton's Bar & Grill and moving into an apartment on H Street before the gastro real estate boom took hold. When it came time for his next venture, setting up a bar with great food close to home seemed like the right move.

The only question remaining was what to serve. A quick trip to his hometown near Cape Cod provided the answer. "I went home and spent about ten days up there eating a lot of seafood," he says. "Then we came up with a menu of simple comfort food with a flair based on the flavors up there."

The wildly popular White Cheddar Lobster Mac & Cheese showcases the original intent of the neighborhood spot. It's simple, crowd-pleasing, and is a nod to Hamilton's and Rhode Island native Chef Graig Glufling's roots. The seafood-infused mac and cheese started out as just a side dish only meant to appear on the menu for a weekend, but customers kept sending word back to the kitchen that it needed to be a permanent Liberty Tree fixture. When attempting to make it at home, really good quality cheese and fresh lobster meat make all the difference.

Much like everything else served at the H Street hangout, the signature dish is made in house. "We make everything from scratch," Hamilton tells. "The only thing we buy is ketchup."

WHITE CHEDDAR LOBSTER MAC & CHEESE

SERVES 6–8

1 pound dried shell pasta
1 stick butter
½ cup all-purpose flour
3 cups heavy cream
2 cups shredded white cheddar
   (Vermont, aged 2 years, if possible)
2 tablespoons mascarpone cheese
2 tablespoons grated pecorino Romano
Salt and pepper

1½ pound lobster, boiled and broken down
   into chunks
2 tablespoons truffle oil
½ bunch fresh chopped parsley (garnish)

For panko topping:

2 cups panko bread crumbs
¼ cup melted butter
¼ cup grated pecorino Romano

Preheat oven to 400°F. Boil salted water and cook pasta until al dente. Drain well and cool under cold running water. Set aside.

Melt butter slowly over medium heat, add flour to make a roux, stirring constantly until flour is incorporated. Cook for 5 minutes on low heat, stirring occasionally to keep it from burning. Add heavy cream, cheddar, mascarpone, and pecorino stirring over medium heat until everything is melted and smooth. Season with salt and pepper. Fold in lobster meat and cooked pasta. Transfer mixture to 8-ounce ramekins. Combine ingredients for panko topping and top the pasta with the mixture. Bake until well browned. Drizzle with truffle oil and fresh chopped parsley.

MANDU

1805 18TH STREET NW
WASHINGTON, DC 20050
(202) 588-1540
MANDUCK.COM
CHEF/CO-OWNER: YESOON LEE
CO-OWNERS: JEAN LEE AND DANNY LEE

The Lee family would sit around the kitchen table and roll dumplings the way others would sit around the den and watch reruns. "When I grew up, it was the way we would wind down our day," says Danny Lee, who along with his mother and sister runs the restaurant Mandu, which means "dumpling" in Korean. "That was our family TV night. The same way we fold them now at Mandu is the way we folded them twenty-five years ago in our kitchen."

Danny's mom, Yesoon Lee, was one of those lives-in-the-kitchen women who always loved to entertain and cook. Today, at sixty-six, Yesoon continues to do what she

loves, putting in many seventy-hour work weeks in the back of the house making Korean dishes, some that have been in her family for generations. "She just started taking off two days a week," her son tells.

One of Yesoon's most requested menu items is her Dolsot Bibim Bap. Danny remembers that when he was growing up, his mom would set out the components of the dish in the kitchen before she went to work so Danny and his sister could put the bibim bap together as an afternoon snack when they came home from school. "The most important part of the dish is the prep," he says. "That's probably true for almost all Korean dishes. Once you do the prep the rest is easy."

The attention to the pre-cooking stages of Mandu's Dolsot Bibim Bap sets it apart from others, Danny says. Each vegetable is prepared and seasoned separately. In order to achieve the authenticity, he recommends investing in stone bowls, which keep the rice dish hot until you reach the bottom.

DOLSOT BIBIM BAP

SERVES 4–6

1 pound beef rib eye
½ cup steamed white rice
1 egg
1½ tablespoons Gochujang sauce per bowl
    of Bibim Bap

Marinade (per 1 pound of beef):

¼ cup soy sauce
2 cloves crushed garlic
2 tablespoons sugar
1 tablespoon red wine
1 tablespoon Korean rice syrup

2 stalks chopped green onion
6 tablespoons sesame oil
Ground black pepper to taste
2 teaspoons roasted sesame seeds
1½ tablespoons salt
Soybean or vegetable oil
3 tablespoons soy sauce

Vegetables:

1 pound fresh spinach
1 pound soybean sprouts
1 pound carrots, peeled
1 pound shiitake mushrooms
1 pound zucchini

To prepare the beef: Combine and mix all the marinade ingredients into a large mixing bowl. Add 1 pound of thinly sliced rib eye and hand-massage the marinade into the beef. Store in refrigerator for at least 2 hours. Remove from refrigerator and massage in 2 tablespoons of sesame oil. Place back in refrigerator for later use.

To prepare the vegetables: Blanch spinach by plunging it into boiling water, then transferring it to a bowl of ice water. Remove from ice bath and lightly press water out. Season with 2 tablespoons sesame oil, 1 teaspoon sesame seeds, and ½ tablespoon salt. Store in refrigerator for later use.

Place sprouts in a pot with 2 cups of water. Once water starts to boil, cover with lid and take off heat and let steam for 5 minutes. Remove from water and season with 2 tablespoons sesame oil, 1 teaspoon sesame seeds, 1 teaspoon salt, and a dash of black pepper. Store in refrigerator for later use.

Cut carrots in half and julienne. Lightly sauté with 1 tablespoon salt and a small amount of soybean or vegetable oil. Let cool and store in refrigerator for later use.

Soak mushrooms for at least 2 hours in water. Strain and julienne. Lightly sauté with 3 tablespoons of thin soy sauce—no oil is needed. Let cool and store in refrigerator for later use.

Cut zucchini in half lengthwise, then thinly slice perpendicular to original cut. Soak in salted water for 10 minutes. Strain water out with cheesecloth, and then lightly sauté in a small amount of soybean or vegetable oil as you did with the carrots. Let cool and store in refrigerator for later use.

To assemble: Scoop ½ cup of steamed white rice into the center of stone bowl, the kind found in most Asian markets.

Place ⅓ cup each of spinach, soybean sprouts, carrots, shiitake mushrooms, and zucchini on top of rice into five equal sections. Take the bowl and black it on a burner range at a high heat.

While the bowl is heating, grill ⅓ cup of the prepared marinated beef by placing thin beef strips on a preheated grill or pan in a single layer. Once cooked and removed from grill, use kitchen shears to cut the strips into small pieces before placing onto the rice.

Lightly dice cooked beef and place it into center of vegetables in the bowl.

Fry one egg sunny-side up and place on top of bowl contents so the yolk is directly in the center.

Quickly drizzle sesame oil along the inner edge of the bowl.

Once rice and oil can be heard steaming, remove from the heat. Place onto wooden bowl holder (again, available at most Asian markets).

Serve with Korean gochujang sauce (a red-bean paste that you can also purchase at most Asian markets).

FOOD COLOR

It's a Korean tradition to have five colors—black, white, yellow, green and red—represented in a single dish. Different theories seem to exist on the why of the colorful custom, but most explanations revolve around the belief that each of the five colors represents a sought-after attribute like wisdom (black) or growth (green). Others purport that each color food benefits a different organ in the body, like the heart (red) or the spleen (yellow), or lungs (white). According to the author of the Beyond Kimchee Korean cooking blog (who writes under the penname Holly), each of the colors represents its own matter of universe and meanings. She goes on to explain, "Black belongs to water meaning wisdom of men. White belongs to gold meaning purity. Yellow belongs to soil meaning center of universe (only kings could wear gold color for that reason). Green is wood meaning spring, property. Red belongs to fire meaning creation and passion. A lot of Korean arts and architectures are based on that belief and even the cuisine is influenced by it. That's why you see so many colors in Bibim bap."

Mandu's Dolsot Bibim Bap also uses all five of the significant colors. The black can be found in the stone of the bowl in which it's served. The spinach and zucchini are the green while the sprouts and egg yolks are yellow. The white of the egg fills the white slot and the red comes from the gochujang sauce, a Korean red-bean paste. A perfect rainbow of flavors.

Marcel's

2401 Pennsylvania Avenue NW
Washington, DC 20037
(202) 296-1166
MARCELSDC.COM
Chef/Owner: Robert Weidermer

Chef Robert Weidermer does not believe in shortcuts, fly-by-night fads, or overnight successes. Instead he subscribes to the school of hard work, attention to the smallest of details, and the cult of blood, sweat, and tears. Weidermer is as much about making sure each piece of silver in his dining room sparkles as he is about making certain his kitchen runs with the precision of an army poised for combat. No doubt his ability to see the big and little pictures together at once, along with his fierce passion for this work and his exceptional talent, have allowed him to create one of the city's best and most well-regarded elegant restaurants in town.

The chef extraordinaire also believes in fostering relationships. When talking about the recent farm-to-table trend, he chuckles. "What were they doing before?" asks the chef who worked on farms as a teenager, doing everything from planting corn to slaughtering pigs. "I know every little farm in the area. I've been buying my goat cheese from the same guy for twenty-five years."

This kind of bond extends to almost every aspect of his three local restaurants, including the people who work at Marcel's. "Most of the staff here have all been with me for years," he says. "The maître d' has been here for thirteen years, the chef de cuisine has been with me for fifteen years, most of the waitstaff has been here for ten to thirteen years, and most of the dishwashers for ten years."

Boudin Blanc with Caramelized Onions & Bacon Lardons

MAKES 30 BOUDINS

1 pound boneless, skinless chicken breast

8 ounces foie gras

5 ounces squab breast (can substitute duck breast)

4¾ cups heavy cream, divided

Salt

3 tablespoons chicken glace (chicken stock that has been reduced until thick and syrupy)

1 tablespoon white truffle oil

2 tablespoons chopped fresh black truffles

2 strands hog casings (enough for 30 boudins)

8 ounces bacon lardons (cut slab bacon into medium dice and cook on the stove until crispy)

Grind chicken, foie gras, and squab breast twice through a meat grinder. Transfer ground mixture to a stainless steel bowl and set bowl into another filled with ice.

Pour ½ cup of heavy cream and 1 tablespoon of salt over mixture and put the bowls in refrigerator to chill for 25 minutes.

Remove bowl with meat mixture and incorporate cream with a rubber spatula. Incorporate an additional 4 cups of cream very slowly, whipping with the rubber spatula, adding a dash of salt and then a little cream. Alternate until the 4 cups of cream have been mixed in. Pass mixture through a tamis or fine-mesh strainer and set aside.

In a bowl, combine chicken glace and remaining ¼ cup cream. Incorporate into meat mixture. Add white truffle oil and fresh chopped truffles and combine.

Tie the end of the hog casing. Stuff meat mixture into the casing with a sausage stuffer or pastry bag. Tie the links with butcher's twine to create 2-inch links. Poach sausages in hot salted water until firm, about 15 minutes. Do not let water boil—water should be kept at 175°F.

Plate and spoon sauce (see below) over boudin blanc. Top with bacon lardons.

Sauce

3 tablespoons unsalted butter, divided

1 white onion, diced

½ cup Madeira

1 cup veal stock

Salt, to taste

Pepper, to taste

In a saucepan over medium heat, add 2 tablespoons butter and then the onion. Cook, stirring, until the onion is caramelized, about 5 minutes. Deglaze with Madeira. Add veal stock and 1 tablespoon of butter. Cook over low heat for 5 minutes. Season to taste with salt and pepper.

Lamb Tenderloins Wrapped in Phyllo Pastry with Baby Carrots, Caramelized Garlic & Cumin Madeira Jus

SERVES 6

For the lamb:

1 tablespoon olive oil for searing the tenderloins

6 lamb tenderloins

1 tablespoon Dijon mustard

6 sheets phyllo pastry

1 cup clarified butter

1 cup fresh spinach, blanched and squeezed

1 cup mushrooms, finely chopped and cooked

For the sauce:

3 shallots

1 carrot

1 stalk celery

5 sprigs thyme

½ bottle Madeira

1 cup lamb glace, made from reduced lamb stock

1 cup demiglace, made from reduced veal stock

1 pinch cumin

For the caramelized garlic:

6 garlic cloves, peeled

¼ cup sugar

For the carrots:

18 each baby carrots

1 bay leaf

½ tablespoon ginger root

1 tablespoon honey

1 teaspoon salt

To prepare the lamb: In a large pan with the olive oil, sear the lamb tenderloins so that they are still rare, about 10 seconds on either side. Cool them down. Cut into thirds and roll in Dijon mustard.

Set out one sheet of the phyllo pastry, brush half with clarified butter, and then fold the pastry in half. Brush the phyllo again, lay two lamb tenderloins down on the phyllo and then put a small amount of spinach in between. Place some mushrooms on top in the middle and spinach on either side of the mushrooms. Top with a third tenderloin, creating a pyramid. Wrap the remaining phyllo around the pyramid, rolling and folding it until it's completely covered. Brush the outside of the roll on all sides. Repeat with the remaining lamb.

To prepare the sauce: Start by chopping the shallots, carrots, and celery. Heat a large saucepot. Lightly sauté the vegetables in olive oil until lightly brown. Add the thyme and Madeira. Reduce the Madeira by two-thirds, then add the lamb glace and demiglace. Reduce until it coats the back of a spoon. Add a hint of cumin, then strain.

To prepare the caramelized garlic: Place 1 cup of peeled garlic cloves into a small sauce pot and fill with water until the cloves are just covered by the water, about 3–4 cups depending on the size of the pot. Bring the water to a boil, then strain the water out of the pot, fill once again with cold water until the cloves are just covered, and bring the water to a boil again. Repeat this series of steps 5 times, keeping the garlic in the water the final round.

In a separate saucepot, place ¼ cup of sugar into the pot and heat on low-medium heat. Swirl the dry sugar regularly until it melts and caramelizes. Once the sugar has turned golden and has melted, add the blanched garlic and half

the water [about 1–2 cups] from the pot into the sugar. After you have added the water, the sugar should harden immediately on the bottom of the pot under the garlic. Keeping the pot on low-medium heat, slowly simmer the sugar and garlic mixture until all of the sugar has dissolved into the water, stirring regularly. Some of the water will evaporate as well, creating a thick, syrupy consistency.

To prepare the baby carrots: Place the carrots in a small sauce pot and fill with cold water until the carrots are just covered, about 5–6 cups depending on size of pot. Add the bay leaf, ginger, honey, and salt to the pot. Bring the water to a boil and allow carrots to cook for 3–4

minutes, or until softened. Remove from water and set aside.

Pre-heat oven to 400°F.

To complete and assemble dish: Heat a large pan on top of the stove on high heat. Place the lamb wrapped in phyllo into the pan and sear on all 5 sides for 1–2 minutes per side. Place seared lamb and phyllo onto a baking sheet and place in oven for 5 minutes. Remove the lamb from the oven and allow to rest for 10 minutes. Slice the lamb using a serrated knife into desired portions, and place on plate with the carrots, caramelized garlic, and lamb sauce.

Masa 14

1825 14th Street NW
Washington, DC 20009
(202) 328-1414
Masa14.com
Executive Chef: Adam Goldman
Chefs/Co-Owners: Richard Sandoval and Kaz Okochi
Sous Chef: Rebecca Hassell

Most kids' memories of summer-camp food center around bug juice, mystery meat, and other tales from the kitchen slop crypt. But for Adam Goldman mealtime during his stint at Boy Scout camp turned out to be a helping of things to come. The Masa 14 chef remembers well the summer when the camp chef outright refused to make meatless grub for the vegetarian campers. Goldman jumped in and started whipping up meat-free eats for the other kids, who otherwise would have had to put those merit-badge skills to work to forage for their next meal. He got the camp-cook equivalent of standing ovation.

"They were lining up for seconds," tells Goldman, recalling the biggest and often unheard-of compliment when it comes to camp meals. Fast-forward a bunch of years and people are still clamoring for additional servings of the chef's creations. Masa 14's brunch ranks as one of the town's most popular offerings. The 14th Street Latin-Asian small-plates restaurant buzzes on the weekends for those who want to come and enjoy its all-you-can-eat and all-you-can-drink brunch menu. The *pan dulce* remains a favorite on the menu and exemplifies the way the restaurant, the brainchild of Chefs Richard Sandoval and Kaz Okochi, marries the two cooking traditions not typically paired together.

Although this recipe has many steps, it's relatively straightforward, and if you follow it through you will get a great final product. The toasting of the spices is an important step in the process and helps bring out the flavors, Goldman tells. Although it sounds involved, all you really need to do is place the spices in a dry sauté pan over a medium-to-high flame for about five minutes. The aroma of the spices will begin to tickle your nose when they are done. Remove the spices from the pan and create the sachet using cheesecloth and tie it with string. If you, like Goldman, were a scout you can choose your favorite knot to tie the string; for the rest of us a bow won't win any new merit badges but will do the trick.

PAN DULCE WITH CHILAQUILES

A STANDARD PULLMAN LOAF WILL YIELD 12–14 PIECES OR 6–7 SERVINGS

For pineapple syrup:

1 star anise
2 cloves
2 black peppercorns
½ inch cinnamon stick
½ ounce ginger, peeled and sliced
2 cups sugar
1 cup water
½ pineapple, diced

For ancho whip:

¼ cup heavy cream
2 tablespoons powdered sugar
¼ teaspoon ancho powder or chipotle puree

For french toast mix:

4 whole eggs
4 ounces milk
¼ teaspoon chai tea powder
¼ teaspoon vanilla extract

1 loaf challah bread
8 tablespoons butter

To prepare the pineapple syrup: Place the spices on a dry baking sheet and toast in a 350°F oven until fragrant and make a sachet with the spices and the ginger.

Place sugar in pot over low heat and slowly caramelize the sugar to a medium-dark caramel. Add water and stir to incorporate and dissolve caramel.

Add sachet and cook until syrup is formed. Add pineapple and cool. Syrup should be thick, but will thin out as juice comes out of fruit overnight.

To prepare the ancho whip: Add all ancho whip ingredients into mixer. Whip cream to stiff peaks. Put aside and chill until needed.

To prepare the french toast mix: Mix all french toast mix ingredients together and chill.

To assemble and serve: Slice challah bread into ½-inch thick pieces. Soak bread slices in french toast mix.

In a non-stick skillet, add the butter and cook bread slices over medium heat until both sides are well toasted and the bread has cooked through.

Cut each slice of toast into three pieces, lightly glaze with pineapple syrup, and place one dollop of the ancho whip on top.

CHILAQUILES

SERVES 2–4 PEOPLE

For salsa verde:

2 ounces chopped yellow onion

1 garlic clove

1½ pound tomatillos

1 Anaheim chili, destemmed and deseeded

4 cups of corn oil plus an additonal 3–4 tablespoons
   to cook the other salsa ingredients

¼ cup heavy cream

2 teaspoons hon dashi

½ bunch cilantro

Salt and pepper

Lime juice to taste

4 tablespoons crumbled spicy chorizo

8 whole eggs, whisked vigorously

Salt and pepper

Corn oil

1 dozen corn tortillas, preferably stale, or left out
   overnight to dry out a bit, quartered or cut into
   6 wedges

1½ to 2 cups salsa verde

Garnishes:

Cotija cheese

Crème fraîche

Cilantro, chopped

To prepare the salsa verde: In a saucepan sauté the tomatillos, and Anaheim chili in a little bit of oil until well caramelized but not burned. Add cream and hon dashi and simmer 5 minutes.

Puree until very smooth and chill the sauce until completely cold. Puree one more time, adding the cilantro, salt and pepper to taste, and lime juice.

To assemble: In a nonstick pan, add crumbled chorizo mix and sauté until until cooked through. Add the eight beaten eggs and salt and pepper to taste.

Coat a large sauté pan generously with corn oil (⅛ inch) and heat on medium-high to high heat. When the oil is quite hot, add the tortillas and fry until golden brown. Remove tortillas to a paper towel–lined plate to soak up excess oil. Sprinkle a little salt on the tortillas. Wipe pan clean of any browned bits of tortilla.

Add 2 tablespoons of oil to pan and bring to high heat again. Add the salsa and let salsa cook for several minutes. Then add the fried tortilla quarters to the salsa. Gently turn over the pieces of tortilla until they are all well coated with salsa. Let cook for a few minutes more.

To serve: Place the scrambled chorizo eggs on a plate, then top with some of the chips cooked in the salsa verde. Add one or two more spoons of the salsa on top, sprinkle with cotija cheese, chopped cilantro, and a drizzle of the crème fraîche.

MATCHBOX RESTAURANT

713 H Street NW
Washington, DC 20001
(202) 289-4441
matchbox369.com
Executive Chef: Shannan Troncoso

The prospect of attempting homemade pasta tends to rattle the nerves of the less kitchen-confident among us (read: me). But Chef Shannan Troncoso assures me that two easy-to-find kitchen tools will make this dish—and all pasta-from-scratch endeavors for that matter—a snap. The first item is none other than a basic kitchen scale, which she says should be used in place of measuring cups to measure out the dry ingredients in this recipe. (Troncoso actually recommends using the scale for all baking and dough endeavors.) The second simple-yet-magical piece of equipment in her bag of tricks is a pasta attachment for your mixer. The attachment will eliminate the need for hand cranking, save you time, and overall, cut down on the sweat equity required to create the dish without compromising the final product.

"I bought one for my mom for Christmas and she loves it," Troncoso says of the accessory. She also sent her this recipe for the roasted butternut squash ravioli recipe that the chef makes at Matchbox. Her mom, Shannon tells, also was somewhat apprehensive about attempting the homemade pasta dish. Now with recipe and attachment in hand, she too is a believer.

Troncoso's love of food stretches back to her childhood and her grandmother in southern Georgia, the matriarch of a large Italian family. "I grew up in small town twenty minutes from the border with Florida," says Troncoso, who trained to be a nurse before moving to Denver to go to culinary school. "There were lots of fresh vegetables, fresh food, and farms. In our community and in our family, people would get together every Sunday. I always liked that and I always loved that food was responsible for that."

The Matchbox Chef has another time-saving tip with the squash. Rather than peel it, you can simply have it roast while you prepare the other ingredients. Cut off the top and bottom off of the raw squash, then cut it in half. Scoop out the seeds and let the squash roast at 350°F while getting other ingredients together.

HOMEMADE BUTTERNUT SQUASH RAVIOLI

MAKES ABOUT 120 RAVIOLI

For mushroom cream sauce:

3 ounces unsalted butter

1 tablespoon minced garlic

½ cup flour

2 cups dry white wine

3 ounces chanterelle mushrooms

1 quart heavy cream

1 cup English peas, shelled

2 tablespoons fresh thyme leaves, chopped

2 tablespoons fresh sage leaves, chopped

2 tablespoons flat-leaf parsley leaves, chopped

1 tablespoon kosher salt

1 teaspoon fresh cracked black pepper

For pasta dough:

3½ cups all-purpose flour

5 large eggs

Pinch of kosher salt

1 ounce water (as needed to moisten dough)

For roasted butternut squash puree:

2–3 whole butternut squash (depending on the size)

Extra-virgin olive oil as needed

For ravioli filling:

1 ounce extra-virgin olive oil

2 tablespoons minced shallots

2 tablespoons minced fresh sage

2 ounces white wine

4 cups roasted butternut squash puree

1 teaspoon kosher salt

1 teaspoon black pepper

1 pound ricotta cheese

3 tablespoons hazelnut oil

For egg wash:

1 egg with 1 teaspoon water, beaten well

To prepare the mushroom cream sauce: Melt butter in a heavy-bottom pot over medium heat. Add garlic and cook approximately 1 minute. Whisk in flour to incorporate into the butter and garlic and form a roux. Deglaze with the white wine, using a whisk to mix wine and roux together. Add chanterelle mushrooms and cold heavy cream. Whisk ingredients to break up the roux (this will result in a smooth sauce without lumps). Add remaining ingredients. Whisk sauce until it comes to a boil and becomes thick. Be careful not to burn it!

To prepare the pasta dough using a KitchenAid mixer: Combine flour and eggs in mixer using paddle attachment. On low speed, add a pinch of salt. Mix for approximately 4 minutes. Slowly add water while dough is mixing. Remove the dough from the bowl and place on a lightly flour-dusted work space. Knead by hand until smooth (approximately 5 minutes). Cover dough with a damp towel and allow to rest for 20 minutes before rolling out.

To prepare the pasta dough by hand: Place flour in a mound on a clean work space. Using your fingers, make a well in the center of the flour. Crack eggs, pinch of salt, and water in a bowl and mix with a fork or whisk. Pour the eggs into the well. Using a fork, gently push the flour into the eggs until combined. Knead dough for approximately 10 minutes until smooth. Cover and allow to rest 20 minutes before rolling out.

To prepare the butternut squash puree: Cut squash in half (I cut off the top and bottom to make them easy to set upright, then slice down

the middle). Using a metal spoon, scrape out seeds and coat the squash with olive oil. Place the squash on a parchment paper–lined sheet tray (cookie tray) with the cut side facing down.

Roast in 350°F oven until tender, approximately 25–30 minutes. Cool. Peel off the skin with your fingers. Puree squash in a blender or food processor until smooth.

To prepare the ravioli filling: In a sauté pan, heat olive oil, shallots, sage, and white wine. Cook until tender. Combine with rest of ingredients in a large mixing bowl with a spatula.

To prepare the ravioli: Cut the dough into workable-size pieces. Attach a pasta roller to KitchenAid mixer (or you can use a traditional hand-cranked pasta roller). Using plenty of flour to keep the dough from sticking to the equipment or to itself, feed the dough through the roller, gradually progressing from the thickest setting to the thinnest. The dough will be thin, but not so thin that you can see through it.

Lay the dough on a flour-covered countertop and cut into 4-inch squares (use a pizza cutter, knife, or a square cutting mold).

Place approximately 2 tablespoons of ravioli filling in the center of each square. Brush egg wash on the edges of the ravioli dough and fold in half diagonally to create a triangle. Pinch edges of ravioli tightly. Don't allow any filling to be visible on the edges, or the ravioli will burst when boiling. Place ravioli on a floured plate or tray.

You can freeze the ravioli and they will last for up to 2 weeks. Once the ravioli are frozen, put them in Ziploc freezer bags.

Ravioli and all fresh pasta cook quickly. The ravioli are done once they float in boiling water, approximately 1½ minutes. Once the pasta is done, finish them in the mushroom cream sauce.

To serve: Plate the ravioli while hot. Drizzle with a little hazelnut oil and sprinkle some fresh sage and thyme on top. Enjoy!

Miriam's Kitchen

2401 Virginia Avenue NW
Washington, DC 20037
(202) 452-8926
MIRIAMSKITCHEN.ORG
DIRECTOR OF KITCHEN OPERATIONS: STEVE BADT

The nonprofit organization Miriam's Kitchen draws inspiration from the Tibetan saying "Compassion is like the moon reflecting on one hundred bowls of water." So it's no wonder the group that feeds and helps thousands each year also named its main fundraiser for the idea wrapped up in those beautiful words. Miriam's Kitchen's annual 100 Bowls of Compassion event raises nearly a quarter of the yearly budget for the group

that provides housing, meals, and other services for some of the city's homeless population.

This recipe for salsa verde comes from a recent 100 Bowls of Compassion that had a Road Trip Across America theme. Held at the National Building Museum, the event featured dishes inspired by the hometown memories of both the guests served at Miriam's Kitchen and the volunteer sous chefs who help create healthy, from-scratch meals every day for those guests. The extensive gourmet menu was made entirely by skilled Miriam's Kitchen volunteers with in-kind donations, allowing an impressive 90 percent of the ticket cost to go directly to supporting the group's homeless guests.

"Recipes like this one (featured at our New Mexico table) highlight the diverse regions of our country," explains Director of Kitchen Operations Chef Steve Badt. "With a peppery bite and a bright acid contrast, this salsa is mild, but can be made spicier by substituting Anaheim chilies for the poblano peppers."

Each day donations of food from local markets, farmers, hunters, fishers, and others get delivered to Miriam's Kitchen and determine what will be created that day. Two professional cooks, along with a steady flow of dedicated volunteers, turn the ingredients into healthy, homemade dishes that they serve to the homeless individuals who come to Miriam's Kitchen to eat and receive other services like legal help or free Metro cards. Volunteers do everything from peeling carrots to scrubbing pots to serving food. No kitchen experience is needed to help out at Miriam's Kitchen, just a good attitude and a commitment to volunteering at least once a month. The payoff can be seen reflected in the faces of both the guests and the volunteers.

Charred Poblano Salsa Verde

SERVES 6

1 large onion
2 poblano peppers
1 jalapeño pepper
Kosher salt to taste
½ cup grape-seed oil or olive oil (a mild olive oil—pure rather than extra-virgin, which is too grassy and bitter) plus extra for coating vegetables
3½ tablespoons apple cider vinegar
Freshly ground black pepper to taste

Heat a heavy-bottom cast-iron pan until it is very hot. Slice the onions into thick rings. Season onions and whole peppers with salt and enough oil to cover evenly and place peppers in the pan in one layer. Roast on all sides until they turn black or a deep golden brown. Don't be afraid to leave them in the pan a little longer than you think you should, but don't let the peppers turn white—this is a sign they are completely burned through. Sear the onions on both sides until they are slightly black or a deep golden brown color.

Place peppers and onions in a bowl and keep covered with tight-fitting plastic wrap. Leave bowl on the countertop, not in the fridge. This allows the peppers and onions to steam until they are soft to the touch, about 10–12 minutes.

Peel, seed, and chop the peppers. Finely chop the onions and add to the peppers.

Add the oil and vinegar to the vegetables. Mix thoroughly. Add salt and pepper lightly, then taste and adjust if necessary.

MITSITAM NATIVE FOODS CAFE

SMITHSONIAN NATIONAL MUSEUM OF THE AMERICAN INDIAN
4TH STREET AND INDEPENDENCE AVENUE SW
WASHINGTON, DC 20560
MITSITAMCAFE.COM
EXECUTIVE CHEF/FOOD & BEVERAGE DIRECTOR: RICHARD HETZLER

Fry bread follows a simple recipe and comes with a complex history. The deep-fried flat bread first came into being on the reservations. It used ingredients like sugar, white flour, and other controversial foods that were introduced by the US government and other outside sources and not previously part of the Native American diet. Yet at the same time fry bread is an almost ubiquitous part of the Native American food culture and found in many a Native American home, with each family often having its own subtle take on the basic formula.

"I compare it to how everyone's grandmother has a meat loaf recipe," says Chef Richard Hetzler, who heads up the kitchen at Mitsitam Native Foods Cafe, housed in the Smithsonian National Museum of the American Indian on the Mall. "Everyone makes it a little bit different. It's a recipe that is hard to mess up."

For his part, Hetzler and his team at the popular museum cafe make about two thousand pieces a day. He recommends topping the fry bread with ground beef and says that those who wish to avoid the deep-frying can try brushing the bread with olive oil and grilling it. The classically trained chef, who has fostered a deep respect for what

LIKE BUTTER: JULIA CHILD'S KITCHEN AT THE SMITHSONIAN

Just a short walk from the Mitsitam Cafe, museum visitors with a foodie side can drool over Julia Child's actual kitchen from her Cambridge home housed at the nearby Smithsonian's National Museum of American History. The room, which served as the backdrop for several of her popular television cooking programs, is a necessary pilgrimage for anyone who owns a dog-eared copy of Child's best-selling *Mastering the Art of French Cooking* and is worth the trip for anyone else who might get a kick out of a true mid-century kitchen.

Highlights include the mortar and pestle the chef purchased in Paris while studying at the Cordon Bleu, the straight razor she used to slash the tops of French bread, and her beloved "Big Garland," the six-burner Model 182 Garland commercial stove she purchased secondhand in 1956. (Child used an electric wall oven, which also is part of the kitchen exhibit, when she cooked on TV, but she always preferred her Garland.)

If you stand very still you can almost hear the onions browning in butter and smell the beef bourguignon simmering on top of the Big Garland.

Bon appétit!

he says are the native roots of most food traditions, sometimes can't believe the success of the Mitsitam Cafe, which he helped launch in 2003 after immersing himself in anything he could get his hands on about native cuisine and culture. It was something of a risky experiment, launching such a specialized cafeteria on the Mall. Now, years later, many consider the cafe, which features food from five different regions, a bigger draw than the museum itself.

"Right before we opened I thought, in six months we'll be serving burgers, pizza, and hot dogs," he says. "Now people like to say that we are a cafe with a museum."

FRY BREAD

MAKES 6 ROUND FLAT BREADS

2 cups all-purpose flour
1 teaspoon baking powder
1 teaspoon salt
2 tablespoons sugar
¾ cup milk, plus more if necessary
Corn or canola oil for deep frying
Sugar mixed with ground cinnamon for topping
   (optional)

Special equipment: Deep-fat thermometer

In a medium bowl, combine the flour, baking powder, salt, and sugar. Stir with a whisk to blend. Mix in the milk to make a stiff dough, adding a bit more milk if necessary. On a lightly floured board, divide the dough into 6 pieces. Form each into a ball, and then roll into disks about ¼-inch thick.

In a Dutch oven or deep fryer, heat 3 inches of oil to 350°F on a deep-fat thermometer. Using a sharp knife, cut an X in the center of each dough disk. Place one disk at a time in the hot oil and cook until golden brown (about 2 minutes) on each side. Using tongs, transfer to a paper towel–lined plate to drain. Keep warm in an oven set to a low temperature while frying the remaining disks.

Serve at once, either plain or sprinkled with cinnamon sugar.

Pizzeria Orso

400 South Maple Avenue
Falls Church, VA 22046
(703) 226-3460
PIZZERIAORSO.COM
Executive Chef: Will Artley

Will Artley believes in the art and humor of making good pizza. The humor is all his own but the artistry comes from intense study with a master pizzailo from the Associazione Vera Pizza Napoletana, a non-profit organization devoted to promoting and protecting "true Neapolitan pizza." The only group of its kind, the VPN certifies pizzailos after they successfully complete a rigorous training in the age-old craft of Neapolitan pizza making and have determined that the individual can perform to the group's high standards. His Thunder Kat meets the VPN's strict criteria for Neapolitan pizza only when cooked in a wood-burning oven—one of the VPN requirements—like the one at Orso but it still tastes delicious when made at home in a conventional oven.

"I am a certified pizzailo from the VPN and also certified in Artisan breads," he tells. "My pizza training was under President of VPN Americas Peppe Miele and master teacher José Barrios."

Artley began cooking long before he ever got his pizza certification. When he was growing up, his mom taught him to make an array of traditional Mexican dishes and from that his love of being in the kitchen was born. He went on to study and graduate from the Culinary Institute of America and worked in many types of restaurants before entering the wonderful world of pizza when he took over the kitchen at Pizzeria Orso in Falls Church. "Today I find my inspiration in local food, my life partner Kimberly, and our four dogs—Levi, Raiyna, Chip, and Todd," he happily tells.

The Thunder Kat Pie

MAKES 1

Pizza dough:

1 cup room temperature water

1 teaspoon salt

3 cups "00" flour ("00" is a classification used in Italy to tell how fine a flour is ground. The 00 flour is highly refined and has the consistency of soft powder.)

½ cup sour starter

2 tablespoons olive oil

Sauce:

1 can of San Marzano tomatoes (Artley, with a smile, holds that there is no replacement for this)

2 teaspoons sea salt

Toppings:

5 ounces salami

4 ounces pepperoni

3 buffala or regular mozzarella

5 each grilled Fresno peppers sliced thinly

To prepare the pizza dough: Combine half the water and salt in a bowl and mix for 2 minutes on the lowest speed. Add half the flour and continue on speed 1 of your mixer with the dough hook for another 2 minute then add starter and mix for 1 minute. Add everything else and mix for 14 minutes. Place the mixed dough in a lightly oiled mixing bowl and allow it to ferment for 3 hours. After three hours it should spring back half way to the touch. At this point you can weigh your dough balls out to 8 ounces and allow it to rest for one more hour.

To prepare the sauce: Hand chop the tomatoes after they are drained (save the liquid). Combine tomatoes and sea salt. Yes, that's it. It's all about the tomatoes.

To assemble: After the dough has rested for an hour, use a rolling pin to roll it out to desired size.

Use a 1-inch rim around the outside of the dough, which will make for a nice sized crust. Assemble the pizza on top of an upside down cookie tray with a light dusting of cornmeal, which allows you to slide the pizza right onto the stone.

Using a large spoon or 2-ounce ladle, spoon the sauce on to the middle of the dough. Keeping the spoon against the dough, use a circular motion to spread the sauce over the dough. Do this until the sauce is lightly spread throughout, stopping an inch before the edge of the pizza dough. Make sure not to spread the sauce all the way to the edge, leave yourself an inch. (If you spread the sauce all the way to the end you will not be able to stretch it without getting your fingers in the sauce and the crust will get weighed down.)

Start by placing the salami first and try to make sure each bite will get just enough. Then follow with the pepperoni, the cheese, and finally the Fresno peppers. Remember with this pizza less is more—too many topping will weigh down your dough and make for a lot of sogginess.

Turn on your oven (with pizza stone in it) as high as it will go, allowing it to preheat for 15 minutes.

Rotate the pizza every 4 minutes until the crust become golden brown.

To serve: When it's done, remove the pizza from the oven and allow it to rest for 4 minutes—the pizza is still cooking during this time. Allow the pizza to cook, slice and serve.

Poste Moderne Brasserie

555 8th Street NW
Washington, DC 20004
(202) 783-6060
POSTEBRASSERIE.COM
Executive Chef: Dennis Marron

The Smoked Trout Rillettes has such strong mid-century roots that it deserves a cameo on an episode of *Mad Men*. Chef Dennis Marron got the inspiration for the dish from his mother, who used to whip together canned fish and butter for cocktail parties back in the day. "She probably got the recipe from some kind of 1960s cookbook," says Marron, adding that growing up he and his sisters would act as the bussers and dishwashers when his parents entertained. "She would often use canned salmon or canned tuna and would use a handheld mixer to whip it."

Marron's version calls for smoked trout rather than the canned tuna or salmon and is a bit more layered than the one he remembers from his childhood. Still it's not a difficult dish to replicate at home. "It is a pretty simple recipe," says the Poste Moderne Brasserie executive chef. "Just make sure you get as many of the bones out as you possibly can."

Smoking the trout isn't that hard, but if you want to save the time and go for the quick fix, the chef says you can sub in store-bought smoked trout, and he adds that you can find some good ones out there now.

Like so many of his colleagues, Marron discovered his love of cooking as a kid in his family home's kitchen. I would often help in the kitchen, we were a large family—five kids—so we all had to help," he tells. "I really enjoyed the social time we had when working in the kitchen. Listening to music while putting away groceries, peeling potatoes, shucking corn . . . I even cleaned soft-shell crabs at the age of eight."

SMOKED TROUT RILLETTES

SERVES 8–12 PEOPLE

8 tablespoons butter (1½ sticks), unsalted, room
   temperature
½ cup finely diced onion
½ cup dry white wine
½ cup cream
2 smoked trout (skin, head, tail, and bones discarded—
   should yield around 8 ounces). It's great if you want
   to smoke your own trout, but you can get some very
   good store bought products. Just make sure you are
   getting it from a reputable source, and keep in mind
   that whole is always best.
Juice and zest of 1 lemon
Salt and white pepper to taste

Add 2 tablespoons of butter to a heavy-bottom
medium-size pot on medium heat. Once the
butter is melted, add onion and sweat until
translucent. Add white wine and cream and
reduce by 25 percent. Add cleaned trout and stir
to incorporate, about 1 minute. Remove warm
trout mixture and place into a food processer,
slowly add butter until incorporated. Zest in
lemon and then add juice. Season to taste. Pulse
to incorporate seasoning. Refrigerate to cool and
then serve.

Serve with crackers as a dip or small scoop on
each cracker as an hors d'oeuvres. It can also be
plated as a composed appetizer.

Proof

775 G Street NW
Washington, DC 20001
(202) 737-7663
PROOFDC.COM
Bar Manager: Adam Bernbach

Adam Bernbach comes to spirits by way of coffee. As a high school student at the Edmund Burke School, he got a job as a roaster at the nearby Sirius Coffee Company, which once stood above the Van Ness Metro station. Working at the indie shop opened up his palate and his imagination. "I had to taste everything and I got very into the flavors in food," says the mixologist who heads up the bar program at both Proof and Estadio. "Over time, through coffee I got into single-malt scotch, and through scotch I got into other spirits, and through spirits I got into cocktails."

Much to his delight, Bernbach has watched the cocktail scene in DC soar. "There's been a real explosion of the cocktail scene here, especially in the past five years," he says. "It's phenomenal. People's tastes are getting more sophisticated."

Customers, he finds, are now more willing to try new combinations and ingredients, a development that has fostered the opportunity for more creativity when it comes to experimenting behind the bar. His "Root" drink on the menu at Proof is a good example of how he puts new spins on classic concoctions. Named for its earthy ingredients and his late mother (whose name was Ruth, which in Hebrew is pronounced, "Rut"), the signature drink combines El Tesoro blanco tequila, Ramos Pinto white port, and Chartreuse. It's finished off with a touch of citrus and served in a coupe glass.

Root Cocktail

MAKES 1 COCKTAIL

1½ ounces blanco tequila
½ ounce Chartreuse
1 ounce white port
Orange zest

To create the cocktail, pour ingredients one at a time over ice and stir well.

Strain the mixture into a coupe glass and garnish with an orange zest.

PS 7's

CLOSED BUT NOT FORGOTTEN AT:
777 EYE STREET NW
WASHINGTON, DC 20001
CHEF/OWNER: PETER SMITH

Chef Peter Smith landed his first kitchen gig at the ripe old age of fourteen. His mom, a photographer, was shooting an event at a local country club and started chatting with the chef there about her son's love of cooking. The next day a teenage Smith started working as an apprentice to that chef. "I spent from seven in the morning to seven at night in the kitchen, and I thought it was the coolest thing ever," says Smith, who clearly was smitten.

Smith's love of cooking was closely aligned to his parents—and his grandmother—even before his mom helped him secure that first job. Like so many others in the field, he remembers fantastic Sunday meals that brought the family around the table. Cooking started first thing in the morning and took up much of the day.

Fast forward almost thirty years later and Smith still spends hours on end creating the dishes that he dreams up in his culinary imagination. This recipe for Pull-Apart Pork Sticky Buns is a case in point and one of the more popular creations to come out of the much-loved but now closed PS 7's.

The idea came to him when one night he was cooking pork at the same time the pastry chef was pulling a batch of "Delecta buns," her deliciously gooey take on cinnamon buns, out of the oven. "It smelled like breakfast," he says. "It was a perfect combination." And after some tinkering around, a recipe was born.

Although it has many steps, Smith promises it's not a complicated undertaking. Just one that takes time. The majority of the time factor goes into cooking the pork, although you don't have to stand over it. "Once you get the pork started, you can then go on a bike ride for three hours," he says. "It's a pretty forgiving recipe. If you go over half an hour or forty-five minutes, probably even an hour, it will be OK. Set it and forget it."

And if you stick with it, your kitchen will smell like breakfast all day.

PULL-APART PORK STICKY BUNS

MAKES APPROXIMATELY 60 MINI STICKY BUNS

For the sponge:

$^2/_3$ cups water
1¼ teaspoon active dry yeast
1 cup bread flour
2 teaspoons sugar

For the dough:

Sponge from recipe above
1 egg
½ cup milk
1 tablespoon milk
1 teaspoon active dry yeast
¼ cup granulated sugar

2½ cups bread flour
1½ teaspoons salt
½ teaspoon baking powder
4 tablespoons unsalted butter

For the syrup:

¼ teaspoon ground allspice
4 tablespoons corn syrup
4 tablespoons melted butter
½ cup brown sugar
¼ teaspoon salt
1 tablespoon water

For the pork filling:

3 pounds very fatty pork butt

1 carrot

1 stalk celery

1 each onion

3 bay leaves

1 small bunch fresh thyme

1 teaspoon black peppercorns

1 teaspoon whole cloves

1 teaspoon whole allspice

1 stick cinnamon

2 quarts water or veal stock

1 tablespoon brown sugar

Salt and pepper, to taste

2 ounces rendered pork fat

To prepare the sponge: Whisk together ingredients and allow the sponge to rest while you gather the rest of your ingredients and make the syrup for the buns.

To prepare the dough: Place all of the ingredients except the butter, wet ingredients first, into the bowl of a KitchenAid mixer fitted with a dough hook attachment. Mix on the lowest speed until mixture is cohesive. Turn mixer up to speed 3, and mix for 4 minutes. Still on speed 3, gradually add the unsalted butter. When butter is incorporated, the dough is done. Place dough in a warm area of the kitchen and allow to rest for about 40 minutes.

To prepare the syrup: Simply mix all of the ingredients until the mixture is smooth.

To prepare the pork filling: Smoke the pork butt for 1 hour on a grill. Place wood chips on top of the coals and off-set the pork butt so it is not directly over the heat. Then place the pork butt, all of the vegetables (roughly chopped), all of the spices, and the water or stock into a 6-quart pot. Cook for approximately 5 hours in a 300°F oven, until the meat is falling apart and tender. Remove the pork from the liquid, strain the liquid, and set aside. Skim fat for later use.

Add the brown sugar to the braising liquid and reduce the braising liquid by 80 percent. Let cool. When the meat and braising liquid are cooled to almost room temperature, place the meat in the bowl of a KitchenAid mixer fitted with the paddle attachment. Mix on first speed until the meat shreds thoroughly and the mixture takes on a moist, spreadable texture. Add salt, pepper, and brown sugar, and stir in the rendered pork fat and braising liquid until you reach a soft, smooth, spreadable consistency.

To assemble: Preheat oven to 350°F. On floured sheet pans, roll dough (it will be sticky) out to ¼-inch thickness and place in freezer. While dough is freezing, spray a 13 x 9 x 2-inch pan with nonstick spray and then carefully spread a thin layer of the syrup over the bottom of the pan. Remove dough from the freezer. Cut into 4-inch-wide strips, and roll slightly more, to even out the thickness if needed. Spread a thin layer of the pork filling onto the rolled dough, and roll up like a cinnamon roll. Cut the rolled up logs into 1 inch wide pieces, and place them on syrup on prepared pan. Bake for a minimum of 10 minutes or until golden. Brush the tops with butter and enjoy.

QUILL

THE JEFFERSON
1200 16TH STREET NW
WASHINGTON, DC 20036
(202) 448-2300
JEFFERSONDC.COM

Calling Quill a hotel bar is like saying the Constitution is a just another legal document or the White House is one more home office. From the moment the top hat–clad doorman ushers you into the historic Beaux Arts hotel, it becomes apparent that you have not arrived just anywhere for a nightcap. The historic boutique hotel stands on 16th Street, just blocks away from the White House, and the clientele who come to Quill reflect the boutique hotel's stately location. Local power players as well as high-profile guests can sometimes be spotted sipping at Quill, engaged in what appears to be intriguing inside-the-Beltway banter, or just soaking up the cocktail culture.

Behind the bar itself, the skilled staff elevates Quill cocktail preparation to an art form. All the mixers here are house-made and expertly blended with herb-infused alcohols. Kentucky Salty Dog remains a Quill favorite and serves as something of its signature cocktail, expertly showing how the bar prides itself on reimagining classic combinations.

If you come in an adventurous mood, consider ordering the "Master Mind," and the mixologist will create a "spontaneous" cocktail just for you.

As an homage to the hotel's presidential namesake, Quill's striking interior is steeped in Jeffersonian images and lore. The eighteenth-century European maps that adorn the walls trace the actual routes the author of the Declaration of Independence took when he traveled through the wine regions of France, Germany, and Italy. Under foot, the parquet flooring recreates the pattern Jefferson, who was also a skilled architect, designed for Monticello's main salon.

KENTUCKY SALTY DOG COCKTAIL

MAKES 1 COCKTAIL

3 grapefruit wedges
2 ounces Bulleit bourbon
1½ teaspoons Aperol
1½ teaspoons grapefruit bitters
1½ teaspoons simple syrup

Add grapefruit wedges and bourbon to shaker and muddle. Add Aperol, bitters, and simple syrup, and shake vigorously. Strain into a salted rocks glass.

Rasika West End

1190 New Hampshire Avenue, NW
Washington, DC 20037
(202) 466-2500
RASIKARESTAURANT.COM/WESTEND
EXECUTIVE CHEF: VIKRAM SUNDERAM

Chef Vikram Sunderam playfully calls his Avocado Banana Chaat "Indian guacamole." The award-winning Rasika chef uses many of the same ingredients in his version as those typically found in guacamole and he even created his Avocado Banana Chaat to be enjoyed in much the same way as its Mexican cousin—served cold and at the start of the meal. The result is a dish that artfully blends authentic Indian flavors with modern tastes.

Chaat is something of a generic term used to describe a whole range of popular savory snacks in India often sold from street carts in the cities and on the beaches. "Chaat is a very traditional way of cooking," says Sunderam. "It means savories. The basic chaat is a bit sweet, a bit tangy, and a bit spicy. We have potato chaat, fruit chaat, chicken chaat, so I thought why not have an avocado chaat."

The first step in this recipe happens not in the kitchen but at the farmers' market or produce aisle, when you go to pick out the avocados. Look for ripe, firm avocados with only a slight amount of give. If they are too soft, the recipe won't turn out as well. Grilling the banana, rather than using it uncooked, adds another level of texture that complements the avocados and other enticing flavors in this chaat.

While Sunderam includes a chutney recipe—and a wonderful one at that—he does say that you can substitute a store-bought one if you are short on time. If you do decide to make the chutney, you can keep it in the refrigerator for a week or two.

Avocado Banana Chaat

SERVES 4

For the tamarind chutney:

4 ounces pound tamarind

2 ounces dates

1 teaspoon freshly grated ginger

2 garlic cloves

½ ounce jaggery (a pure, unrefined, whole sugar)

2 tablespoons sugar

2 whole red chilies

2 bay leaves

½ teaspoon fennel seeds

¼ teaspoon roasted cumin powder

¼ teaspoon red chili powder

¼ teaspoon black salt

Salt to taste

2 ripe but firm avocados

½ cup chopped onions

½ cup chopped tomatoes

1 teaspoon roasted cumin powder

½ teaspoon red chili powder

¼ teaspoon black salt

4 tablespoons tamarind chutney

2 ripe but firm bananas

2 tablespoons chopped fresh cilantro

Black pepper to taste

To prepare the tamarind chutney: Put all the ingredients except cumin, chili powder, and salts in a heavy-bottom pan. Add enough water to cover the ingredients. Let the mixture boil and then simmer till the dates and tamarind are soft and mashed. Pass the mixture through a fine strainer. Season the extract with the roasted cumin powder, red chili powder, black salt, and salt. Cool and keep aside.

Use 4 tablespoons for the recipe and keep the rest refrigerated.

To assemble: Cut the avocado into quarter-inch dice. Add the rest of the ingredients, except the bananas and cilantro, in a bowl and mix well. Mix in 4 tablespoons of tamarind chutney.

Cut the banana in half and then cut lengthwise and grill on a skillet. Season with salt and black pepper.

Arrange the banana on top of the avocado and garnish with chopped fresh cilantro. Serve cold.

Red Hook Lobster Pound Food Truck

@LobstertruckDC
redhooklobsterdc.com
President (aka King Lobstah Kahuna): Leland Morris
VP Human Resources and Queen of Company Culture (aka The
Lobstah Lady): Robyn Povich

True story. A woman once passed out when she finally got up to the window at the Red Hook Lobster Pound truck. Thankfully she came to in time to order and eat her lobster roll. Such is the power of the lobstah.

The city's most popular and at times faint-inducing food truck brings the taste of Maine to DC by way of Brooklyn. There, Susan Povich and her husband Ralph Gorman came up with the idea to drive up to Maine, fill a truck with lobsters, and sell them back in New York at an empty storefront. Hundreds of pounds went in hours. After a while she started making lobster rolls that sold at flea markets with equal fervor. At that point she asked her Washington-based cousin, Doug Povich, if he wanted to bring the business down here. Doug, teamed up with his friend, the Culinary Institute of America graduate Leland Morris, and a food truck was born.

"Every summer my family would go up to Maine," says Doug, a telecom lawyer, proving once again that everyone in DC is really a lawyer. "We'd have lobster rolls every

day. Sometimes twice a day. Our roll is a distillation of what we thought were all the best lobster rolls we would have up in Maine."

The recipe for the roll that sometimes commands a line two hundred people long is a well-guarded secret, but part of the appeal, Doug reveals, is in the mayo. Red Hook uses house-made mayo that Susan makes up in New York. "It's lemon-based and very light," he tells.

While you have to queue up to get the real deal from the truck, Red Hook's recipe for steamed whole lobster is a good start for those who want to try and re-create the magic at home. One lobster will do if you make it at home, but think about this. The truck goes through thousands of pounds of lobster meat every week (they bring them down about two or three times a week) and it takes about eight lobsters to get one pound of meat, a statistic that could make anybody a bit weak in the knees.

LOBSTER ON THE GRILL

SERVES 4

4 live Maine lobsters, 1½–2 pounds each

4 cloves fresh garlic

10 sprigs of thyme

4 lemons

1½ pounds salted butter, cut into cubes

Coarse sea salt, to taste

1 cup dry white wine

4 sheets heavy-duty aluminum foil

Fire up your grill. The lobster truckers prefer using a natural lump, hardwood charcoal. You want the high flames to subside, leaving a nice, hot bed of burning coals.

Kill the lobsters by placing the tip of a chef's knife about 2 inches back from the eyes on the top of the head of the lobster and driving the knife down through the head until it hits the cutting board. The blade of the knife should be facing the eyes and the bolster of the knife should be pointed toward the tail. Roll the blade of the knife down so that the blade cuts between the eyes and through the shell completely.

After killing the lobsters, place them back in the fridge for about 15 minutes.

Prepare your garlic by smashing the cloves with your knife and removing the outer skin. Then mince the garlic.

Prepare your thyme by pulling the leaves from the stems. Give the thyme a rough chop. Mix the chopped garlic and thyme together.

Cut your lemons in half and set to the side.

Remove the lobsters from the fridge and prepare them for grilling. Take each lobster and hold it with its belly facing up. Using a chef's knife, cut the lobster lengthwise from head to tail, cutting through the body, meat, and through the back shell. It helps to start by placing the tip of the knife where the tail meets the body and rolling the blade down to cut the tail in half (lengthwise) first. Then reverse the motion and cut the body and head in half.

Remove the tomalley and any roe and reserve for other recipes, or discard it.

Remove the rubber bands from the claws.

Place each half lobster on a sheet of foil, belly up.

Place a few cubes of butter down the length of the lobster, being sure to cover the tail. Sprinkle the fresh garlic, thyme, and sea salt down the length of lobster.

Sprinkle the wine down the length of the lobster.

Wrap the lobsters individually in the foil sheets. The wrap should be tight with closed ends, so the ingredients stay in the foil and on the lobster. Place the wrapped lobsters on the grill, belly-side up, for about 9–12 minutes.

Place remaining butter in a small pot and place on the side of your grill to melt.

Dip the cut side of each half lemon in butter and place, cut side down, on the grill.

Remove the lobsters from the foil and turn belly-side down, and grill for an additional 3–5 minutes. Try to keep the melted butter and other liquids released during cooking in the foil instead of falling on the burning coals. This will help prevent a flare-up and the resulting soot from getting on the lobster. You want to finish cooking the meat and get some nice grill marks on the flesh of the tail. You also want to caramelize the garlic and thyme.

The lobsters are finished cooking when the meat is opaque. Adjust your grilling time after you remove the lobster from the foil, if necessary. Larger lobsters will require more time. Also, large claws require more cooking time. Adjust by moving the tail portion of the lobster off the center of the grill for less direct heat with the claws over more direct heat.

Check your lemons. Pull them off the grill when nicely browned on the cut side. You do not need to flip your lemons.

Let the lobsters rest for 5 minutes before eating.

Pour the melted butter in a bowl.

Arrange the grilled lobsters and lemons on a platter.

Enjoy with friends and a cold root beer!

Remember, have fun! Try this recipe with your favorite herbs and flavorings. In our opinion, lobster is best when prepared simply allowing the natural flavor of the lobster to shine through.

RESTAURANT EVE

110 SOUTH PITT STREET
ALEXANDRIA, VA 22314
(703) 706-0450
RESTAURANTEVE.COM
CHEF/CO-OWNER: CATHAL ARMSTRONG

Chef Cathal Armstrong's elegant bouillabaisse comes to his Northern Virginia kitchen by way of both Ireland and France. The Restaurant Eve chef fondly recalls his father, a man he calls "a great natural cook," preparing the dish when he was growing up in Ireland. Armstrong also vividly remembers sampling the fish stew in the south of France, where the dish originated. There, each component—the steamed fish, the sauce, the vegetables—came served on its own plate. A visual nod to its intricate flavors that makes this bouillabaisse among his favorite things to eat.

"What I love about bouillabaisse is the layers and layers of complex flavors," he says. "When I eat it it's almost taxing on my mind."

Fortunately for those re-creating Armstrong's beloved bouillabaisse at home, the process doesn't have to be taxing or complicated. Prepping all the ingredients before you begin the recipe will keep you organized, focused, and leave less room for error. "It's not a difficult dish to prepare," Armstrong reassures. "If you do all the preparation in advance—cut all of the vegetables, have all the seafood washed, and have the stock and saffron ready—then it's only about twenty minutes of prep and about fifteen minutes of cooking to have a great healthy delicious meal on the table."

But before you even get to the stage of prepping the ingredients, you first need to make sure you've purchased the finest ones around. "The best piece of advice Armstrong's

can give about bouillabaisse is to invest in the best ingredients you can source," the chef adds. "The dish in the end will only be as good as its parts. We don't serve it in winter when basil and tomatoes are not in season. It always comes back to the ingredients."

Bouillabaisse

SERVES 4

For the broth:

1 fennel bulb, roughly chopped
2 leeks, roughly chopped
1 head garlic, roughly chopped
8 shallots, roughly chopped
¾ cup olive oil
1 tablespoon saffron
3 large vine-ripened tomatoes, roughly chopped
2 tablespoons tomato paste
2 pounds white fish bones, cleaned, all blood removed
3 quarts water
2 bay leaves
1 bunch fresh thyme (about 1½ cups)
1 bunch fresh parsley (about 1½ cups)

For the rouille:

1 Idaho potato, peeled and cut in large dice
1 cup of the broth from above
2 egg yolks
2 cloves garlic
½ roasted red pepper
2 teaspoons harissa (a Tunisian hot chili paste than can be purchased in most markets)
1 cup olive oil
Salt to taste

To finish the bouillabaisse:

½ fennel bulb, diced
1 leek, washed and diced
2 cloves garlic, peeled and chopped
½ cup olive oil
1 Idaho potato, peeled and diced
1 large, vine-ripened tomato, peeled, seeded, and diced
12 littleneck clams
16 mussels
4 large prawns
1½ pounds cleaned boneless, skinless white fish like cod, rockfish, snapper, or monkfish
Salt to taste
3 tablespoons chopped basil
1 lemon

For garnish:

Slices of baguette, tossed with olive oil and toasted

To prepare the broth: Over a low heat, sweat the fennel, leeks, garlic, and shallots in the olive oil until tender. Add the saffron and continue to cook for another minute. Increase the heat to medium-high and add the tomatoes and tomato paste and cook for 2 more minutes, stirring constantly. Add the fish bones, water, bay leaves, thyme, and parsley, bring to a simmer, and cook for 45 minutes. Strain and set aside.

To prepare the rouille: Cook the potato in 1 quart of the broth until it is tender, then strain and reserve the liquid (you may need it to thin the rouille later). In a food processor, place the potato, egg yolks, garlic, roasted pepper, and harissa. Turn on the processor and add

the olive oil in a thin stream as you would for mayonnaise. Season to taste. (The rouille should have the texture of mayonnaise; you can use the reserved broth to thin if needed.)

To finish: In a large braising pan, sweat the fennel, leeks, and garlic in the olive oil until tender. Add the potato and continue to sweat until it is tender. Add the tomato, clams, and the remaining broth from above, increase the heat to medium, and cook until the clams start to open. Add the mussels, prawns, and white fish and continue to cook until all of the seafood is just cooked. Season the bouillabaisse, add the basil, and squeeze the juice from the lemon. Serve with the rouille and toasted baguette slices on the side.

RIPPLE

3417 CONNECTICUT AVENUE NW
WASHINGTON, DC 20008
(202) 244-7995
RIPPLEDC.COM
EXECUTIVE CHEF: LOGAN COX

Don't worry if you spot Chef Logan Cox picking the leaves off trees near his Cleveland Park restaurant. He hasn't been hitting the cooking sherry or been spending too much time standing over boiling stockpots. What you have stumbled upon is just Cox collecting ingredients for tonight's dinner menu. And, no, you need not worry about that either.

Cox is one of a growing number of chefs worldwide embracing the practice of hyper-local wild foraging. "Most mornings I wake up an hour earlier than I need to and forage," explains the Petworth resident. "Some days I go down to Rock Creek Park where it's more lush, but once you know what you are looking for you start to see it everywhere."

And, he does mean everywhere. Cox has collected food everywhere from cracks in the sidewalk to the side of the road. Wild dandelions, ramps, and different sorrels are some of the ingredients Cox finds in these and other places around town to bring back to the Ripple kitchen. The pine needles he uses in this recipe to smoke the arctic char fillets typically come from Ordway Street right around the corner from Ripple. Cox, who cites the book *Stalking the Wild Asparagus* as one of his inspirations, calls foraging the ultimate locavore moment. "Food," he adds, "really is everywhere."

If you want to attempt smoking the fillets with the aroma of the pine needles, the first step is to soak them in warm water overnight, tells the chef who started college on a football scholarship and plays the bass. You can create a makeshift smoker, if you don't own one, by using deep metal pans, placing one inside another. If you can't find pine needles, rosemary works as a substitute.

Red Russian Kale Salad, Anchovy Dressing, Toasted Couscous, Pickled Potatoes & Smoked Arctic Char Rillettes

SERVES 6

For the anchovy dressing:

5 egg yolks
1 egg
Juice of two lemons
Juice of two limes
5 anchovy fillets
7 garlic cloves, peeled and finely chopped
¼ pound Parmesan cheese, finely grated
7 ounces of olive oil
3½ ounces finely diced red onion
2½ ounces finely chopped chives
2½ ounces yellow mustard seed
Pinch of salt, to taste

For the smoked arctic char rillettes:

1 handful of pine needles
1 bunch sage
3 sprigs rosemary
2 fillets artic char
1 cup crème fraîche
Pinch of chives
2 teaspoons kosher salt

For the couscous:

1 cup Israeli couscous:
2 teaspoons kosher salt
1½ cups water
1 teaspoon of olive oil

For pickled potatoes:

10 fingerling potatoes, thinly sliced ¼ inch thick on a mandoline and rinsed of excessive starch
3½ ounces white wine vinegar

10½ ounces water
¾ ounce of kosher salt
2 bay leaves
¹/₃ ounce mustard seed
4 whole cloves

1 head Red Russian kale, washed and removed of fibrous stems

To prepare the anchovy dressing: In a blender combine the yolks, egg, lemon and lime juices, anchovies, garlic, and Parmesan. Blend till smooth. While blender is still running slowly drizzle in the olive oil until dressing is thick, creamy and emulsified. Pour the dressing into a bowl and mix in the remaining ingredients.

To prepare the arctic char rillettes: Add pine needles, sage, and rosemary to a smoker. Place arctic char fillets over smoking herbs and needles until fully cooked. This is known as a "hard smoke," meaning that the temperature of the smoke needs to be high enough to also cook the fish completely. The smoking process should only take around 6 minutes.

Reserve char and let rest to room temperature.

Add room temperature char, crème fraîche, chives, and salt to a KitchenAid mixer bowl with the paddle attachment. Paddle the mixture on medium speed until well incorporated. The mixture should be spreadable, or have the consistency of rillettes or resemble a nicely textured puree.

To prepare the couscous: In a 350°F oven toast the couscous by itself on a sheet pan till golden brown. Remove from oven and let sit until room temperature.

In a small saucepan bring salt, water, and olive oil to a boil. Add the toasted couscous to the boiling water, immediately turn the heat down to low, and cover with a lid. The couscous should be ready in 12–15 minutes. Reserve and chill.

To prepare the pickled potatoes: Remove sliced fingerling potatoes from rinsing water, place in a bowl big enough to hold the potatoes, and the hot pickling liquid. In a small sauce pot bring vinegar, water, salt, bay leaves, mustard seed, and cloves to a boil. Once liquid is boiling, pour over top of the fingerling potatoes. Chill potatoes in the pickling brine over night to completely infuse the brine.

To plate: In a small bowl add a spoonful of dressing to a salad bowl, gently toss the kale to evenly coat the greens. (It's always best to start with too little dressing; you can always add more if desired.) Add the couscous and pickled potatoes to the same bowl and mix gently for even distribution.

On a plate place a long smear of Smoked Artic Char Rillette with an off set spatula or spoon. Using the smear as a guide gently place the now dressed salad in a line next to the rillette being sure to leave the rillette exposed.

Composed Seasonal Vegetable Salad, Goat Yogurt, Cardamom & Charred Lettuce Puree

This is a salad that we have on our menu at Ripple every day. We purchase 95 percent of our produce from surrounding organic farmers, growers, and foragers. This dish allows us to showcase all the great things our area has to offer, sometimes found directly in our backyards. The treatment of the vegetables is based on how the vegetable is that day—some are roasted, others blanched, others braised, some pickled, and others served raw. The preparations change daily.

SERVES 6

For the charred lettuce puree:

Handful of leek tops
½ pound salad or other greens
½ pound vegetable stems and tops
1 yellow onion, julienned
1 cup water
4 tablespoons unsalted butter
Salt to taste

For the cardamom vinaigrette:

½ cup red wine vinegar
10 cardamom pods, smashed to expose
    the interior seeds
1⅓ cups olive oil
Salt to taste
¼ cup goat yogurt in a squeeze bottle
2 sprigs nasturtium (optional)
2 sprigs baby dandelion (optional)
2 sprigs chickweed (optional)
2 sprigs fennel fronds (optional)
2 sprigs lemon balm (optional)
2 sprigs pea shoots (optional)
2 sprigs purslane (optional)

To prepare the charred lettuce puree: In a 400°F, oven place the leek tops, greens, stems, and vegetable tops on a sheet tray. Roast in oven till all items are black, charred, and brittle. You cannot overcook this—the idea is to essentially burn the vegetables.

In a small saucepan, place the onion, water, butter, and salt and simmer until the onions are meltingly tender. Remove from heat.

Place the stewed onions in the blender with the charred vegetables, puree until smooth and spreadable, season with salt to taste. Chill.

To prepare the cardamom vinaigrette: In a small sauce pan add the red wine vinegar and cardamom pods, reduce by half. Remove from heat and let chill to room temperature. Place cooked vinegar in a mixing bowl and whisk in olive oil. Season with salt to taste. Reserve.

To plate: On a plate, place a smear of the charred lettuce puree off to the side with an offset spatula. In a small salad bowl add the cardamom vinaigrette and one portion of the vegetables with a pinch of salt, coat evenly. Decoratively place the vegetables in a natural fashion. Place goat yogurt in a squeeze bottle and place small dots in and around the vegetables. Garnish the now-plated vegetables with decorative greens and herbs such as nasturtium, baby dandelion, chickweed, fennel fronds, lemon balm, pea shoots, and purslane.

Sugar Magnolia

3417 Connecticut Avenue NW
Washington, DC 20008
rippledc.com
(202) 244-7995
Pastry Chef: Alison Reed

Allison Reed found her way to Sugar Magnolia, the tiny bakery storefront attached to the restaurant Ripple, through Craigslist. The classically trained pastry chef replied to the post and the rest is butter and sugar history.

"I had been here countless times and was in love with it, so when the ad for a pastry chef came up on Craigslist I was thrilled," tells Reed, who does double duty as the pastry chef at Ripple and Sugar Magnolia. "[They] told me about the idea to do ice cream sandwiches in the market, which happens to be one of my favorite things to make. I had to be a part of it."

Reed is not only part of it, she is an integral part of it, getting rave reviews for her baked goods and those from-scratch ice cream sandwiches that sold her on the gig. Including treats for those customers who cannot eat gluten felt important to Reed, who wants everyone to be able to come in and pick something up from the happy turquoise, red, and white shop. Ripple and Sugar Magnolia are big gluten-free spots," she tells. "I have about six things in our market that are gluten-free."

Gluten-Free Chocolate Financier

(MAKES 12–16 MINI MUFFINS)

6 ounces (1½ sticks) butter
4 ounces dark chocolate (70 percent), melted
2 cups ground almond flour
6 tablespoons cocoa powder
¼ teaspoon salt
1½ cups confectioners' sugar
5 ounces white chocolate pieces, finely chopped
5 egg whites

Add egg whites, chocolate, and butter slowly to bowl and mix until combined.

Scoop your batter into desired molds (a mini cupcake pan works best). Bake for about 15–20 minutes, or until a skewer comes out clean.

Preheat the oven to 325°F. Brown the butter in pot by melting over a medium heat and continuing to let it cook until there is a very nutty aroma and the butter has become light brown in color. Set aside.

Melt chocolate over a double boiler. Set aside.

Mix almond flour, cocoa powder, salt, sugar, and white chocolate pieces in bowl of mixer with a paddle attachment.

RIS

2275 L Street NW
Washington, DC 20037
(202) 730-2500
RISDC.COM
Chef/Owner: Ris Lacoste

Ris Lacoste speaks the way she cooks: with kindness, warm details, and without the slightest hint of pretense.

The chef and owner of this West End restaurant approaches the business with a studied but gentle touch and a passion for feeding others that was passed on by her mother. "There were seven of us and my father and we had three hot meals a day," says Lacoste, who was born Doris but hasn't been called that in many years. "We ate at five o'clock every single day and my mother made everything."

One of the most beloved dishes of many well-loved dishes back in the day in the Lacoste family was her mom's Chicken Pot Pie, which now graces the menu at her restaurant. "My mom used to make it in a Pyrex baking dish and would line it with her own pie crust that she made with lard. We would fight over crust leftover in the bottom of the dish."

Lacoste has tweaked the savory pie slightly from her mother's version but the soul of the dish remains intact. When making this wonderfully comforting family recipe at home Lacoste stresses the importance of cooking the filling and crust together at the same time. "It's crucial to bake the pastry with the filing," she says. "The crust and filling have to talk to each other."

Although Lacoste enjoyed being in her mom's kitchen and worked at a butcher shop and restaurants throughout high school and college, her career path in cooking didn't take shape until after graduation. She began her studies at the University of Rochester as pre-med but ultimately graduated with a degree in French from the University of California at Berkeley. From there she went to Paris with the idea of becoming a translator for the UN. A series of serendipitous twists and turns led her to enroll at the Anne Willan's La Varenne École de Cuisine, and thus began her storied culinary career, which began in France. There she met greats like Julia Child (years later she had the honor of preparing dinner for Child on her 90th birthday) and in time Lacoste landed on L Street at the pretty, light-filled restaurant that bears her name.

CHICKEN POT PIE

Chef's note: "In my humble opinion, there should always be plenty of light, flaky crust in a chicken pot pie. At my house we would fight over my mother's flaky pastry lining the bottom of the Pyrex baking dish. Make plenty of your favorite pie dough or buy 100-percent butter puff pastry, rolled to ⅛ inch and cut to cover and/or encase individual ramekins or larger casseroles."

Pie Dough:

2 cups all purpose flour (Ris uses King Arthur)

¾ tablespoon salt

1/3 pound pure lard

You can make your own pie dough or buy 100-percent butter puff pastry, rolled to ⅛ inch and cut to cover and/or encase individual ramekins or larger casserole dishes.

For the roux:

4 ounces butter

1 cup flour

For the filling: (makes 3-4 quarts, 6-8 servings)

8 ounces mushrooms, whole or quartered (if large)

1 cup pearl onions, peeled

Salt and freshly ground pepper

Fresh thyme

Olive oil

2 tablespoons butter

1 large onion, diced, about 2 cups

2 large stalks celery, cut in large dice, about 1 cup

2 carrots, cut in large dice, about 1 cup

2 tablespoons chopped fresh thyme

2 tablespoons chopped fresh sage

2 quarts chicken stock

1 bay leaf

1 large potato, cut in large dice, about 1 cup

1–2 cups, or to taste, root vegetables that are available: parsnip, celery root, sweet potato, or all of the above, peeled and cut in large dice

1 cup fresh or frozen English peas

2 cups roasted chicken meat, cut in large dice or shredded chunks

Sherry vinegar

Roll out the pastry to suit your needs and keep covered in the refrigerator until ready to use.

To prepare the roux: Melt the butter in a heavy-based saucepan over medium heat. Whisk in the flour, stirring constantly, spreading the paste over the bottom of the pan to lightly color and cook the flour, about 5 minutes. Set aside in a warm place until ready to use.

To prepare the filling: Roast the mushrooms and pearl onions in a 350°F oven until golden. Season with salt and pepper, fresh thyme, and olive oil. Set aside when done until ready to use.

In a heavy-based, 2-gallons soup pot or Dutch oven, melt the 2 tablespoons of butter and add the diced onions, celery, and carrots. Sprinkle with the chopped thyme and sage and cook until the onions are barely soft, stirring occasionally, just enough to release the aromatics from the vegetables, about 5 minutes. Add the chicken stock and bay leaf and bring to a boil. Let simmer for another 5 minutes to meld the flavors and season the stock.

Add the potatoes and any additional root vegetables. Season lightly with salt and fresh cracked pepper. Bring just to a boil and add the peas, roasted mushrooms, roasted pearl onions,

and chicken meat. Bring back just to a boil again, keeping in mind that you have about 5 minutes to finish from the point of adding the potatoes before they are overcooked.

Thicken with the roux, whisking in a bit at a time and dissolving each bit, avoiding lumps. Taste for seasoning and adjust with salt, pepper, and a dash of sherry vinegar for brightness. Let cook a minute longer and remove from the heat.

To finish: Prepare your pastry to accommodate your vessel. Fill with the pot pie filling and cover with more pastry. Filling can be hot if put in the oven immediately or chilled and can be kept in the refrigerator until ready to use. Cooking time will be in a 350°F oven, but will depend on size of pie and whether or not filling was hot or cold. Individual portions take 20 minutes or so. Larger casseroles may take up to 1 hour or longer.

RIS WALKS 60

Every day at noon Chef Ris Lacoste peeks out the front door of her restaurant to see who has come. Since New Year's Day 2012, the chef has committed herself to walking for an hour every weekday and has invited anyone who wants to come along with her. And they do.

Lacoste loves the company and knowing that others count on her to be there helps the chef step away from her busy life and exercise outside. The only thing Lacoste asks in exchange is that her walking companions donate a dollar for each mile they walk together, which she then adds to and donates to the Women's Heart Center at nearby George Washington University Hospital. The chef began her RIS Walks 60 effort after suddenly losing her beloved mother, Yvonne Lacoste, to heart disease. "As a chef I realize I'm in the position not only to feed people fresh, whole foods, but also to walk with them on the path to better health," she says.

Butterscotch Pudding

SERVES 6

½ cup plus 3 tablespoons dark brown sugar, packed

3 tablespoons water

1¾ cups whole milk

½ cup heavy cream

¼ cup arrowroot

¼ teaspoon salt

3 egg yolks

3 tablespoons butter, unsalted, at room temperature and cut into 4 pieces

2 teaspoons vanilla extract

2 tablespoons light rum

Fresh whipped cream

Have six 3–4 ounce serving cups ready. (At RIS the pudding is served in martini glasses.) You will pour the pudding into them.

In a medium, heavy-bottom saucepan, put in the ½ cup brown sugar and water over medium heat and bring to boil. Stir to dissolve sugar, and boil for 2 minutes. Lower heat if necessary.

Add 1½ cups of the milk and all of the cream and bring to boil. Do not worry if the mixture curdles as it heats.

While milk is heating, put the arrowroot and salt into food processor and pulse. Pour mixture out of processor into small bowl, set aside.

Put the 3 tablespoons of brown sugar and yolks into the processor and blend for 1 minute. Scrape down sides of bowl with spatula, add remaining ¼ cup of milk and pulse to blend. Add the arrowroot and salt mixture to processor and pulse a few times.

With the machine running, very slowly pour in the hot mixture from the saucepan. Process for a few seconds and then pour everything back in saucepan.

Over medium heat, whisk constantly, making sure to get the edges of the pan, until pudding thickens and a few bubbles come up to the surface (about 2 minutes). You do not want the pudding to boil but you want it to thicken, so lower your heat if needed.

Scrape pudding back into processor. If you have a scorched spot in pan, avoid scraping it. Pulse a few times.

Add the butter, vanilla, and rum and pulse until all are evenly blended.

Pour pudding into cups. If you do not want skin to form on top, press a piece of plastic wrap against the surface of each pudding to create an airtight seal. Or you can cover the top of each cup with plastic wrap.

Refrigerate at least 4 hours before serving. (Covered pudding can be refrigerated up to 2 days.) Before serving, top each cup of pudding with fresh whipped cream.

Room 11

3234 11th Street NW
Washington, DC 20010
(202) 332-3234
room11dc.com
Chef/Partner: Benjamin "Ben" Gilligan
Partners: Nick Pimentel, Paul Ruppert, and Dan Searing

Something about the corner of 11th and Lamont Streets always called out to Ben Gilligan. Long before businesses started gravitating to that part of Northwest DC, the look and energy of the spot grabbed his attention. "I always liked the way it sat on the block, both unassuming and welcoming," he recalls. "It's not like I dreamed of opening a place there, I just thought it would be a good spot for something."

As what can either be described as foreshadowing or coincidence, or perhaps a touch of both, a storefront opened up on that fateful corner just as Gilligan, who had been working as an art handler, started getting the itch to come back to cooking after a ten-year hiatus. "I missed the pace of the kitchen," tells Gilligan, who worked as a cook in Australia where he spent much of his childhood. "It gets in your bones a little bit."

His background in construction and cooking made the Room 11 co-owner perfectly poised to open what turned out to be a little neighborhood wine bar with an everyone-knows-your-name vibe. "Someone once referred to it as a great, pinky-down wine bar," he shares.

Gilligan acted as general contractor for the project and along with his partners, staff, and friends did most everything, from laying the beautiful floors on up. The floors, a rustic work of art by themselves, Gilligan crafted from reclaimed yellow pine strips he found and cut into three-quarter-inch pieces to look almost like bricks. It's worth casting your eyes down when you walk in to soak up the handiwork and craft beneath your feet. He also helped put in the zinc bar. "I love old zinc," he says. "But it's like a brand new pair of Chuck Taylors at first. They are so clean it's embarrassing. But then they wear over with time."

A true jack-of-all-trades, Gilligan also was a member of the band French Toast playing guitar, bass, and drums in addition to singing for the group that put out a couple of records on a local label. He also played guitar on the album Dust Galaxy, a side-project of Rob Garza's Thievery Corporation. "I have a philosophy degree so I have to do lots of different things," he jokes. "Not many jobs out there for philosophers."

Charred Cauliflower Salad
with Garlic Confit & Tahini Dressing

SERVES 4–6

1 head garlic, plus 3 cloves for tahini dressing,
    peeled and left whole

1 bay leaf

1 sprig thyme

1 cup extra-virgin olive oil

2 lemons, zest and juice

½ cup tahini (sesame paste)

½ teaspoon smoked paprika

Salt and pepper

1 head cauliflower

½ cup vegetable stock or water

1 large bunch curly parsley

For the confit of garlic: Preheat oven to 225°F. Separate garlic head into cloves and peel the cloves. Place the peeled garlic into a small ovenproof saucepan with the bay leaf and thyme, cover with olive oil. Gently heat the saucepan until the garlic is just starting to show color. Place the saucepan on a low rack in the oven. Cook for 4 hours, or until the garlic is a nice warm brown. Remove from the oven and let cool completely. You can jar it now and it will keep for up to a month in the fridge.

For the tahini dressing: Combine the zest of 1 lemon and the juice of 1½ lemons (keep the other half for finishing), the 3 reserved garlic cloves, tahini paste, paprika, and a good pinch of salt and pepper in a food processor. Blend until smooth. Thin with up to ⅓ of a cup of warm water if the dressing seems too tacky. Taste for seasoning. It should be quite lemony and a little salty.

For the charred cauliflower: Turn the oven up to 475°F and heat a sheet pan on the top rack. Chop the cauliflower into bite-size florets or, for a more dramatic effect, cut them into large wedges as you would iceberg lettuce. Toss with just a little of the garlic confit oil. You want the cauliflower to char not fry, and avoid using the actual garlic cloves as they will burn. Spread cauliflower on the hot sheet pan and place in the oven for 8 minutes. Leave it alone. Let it stick to the pan.

After a full 8 minutes, shake the pan to get everything moving. Cook for a further 7 minutes.

Remove pan from the oven and transfer the cauliflower to a large serving dish. Season with a little salt while it is still warm. Heat the sheet pan on the stovetop as you would when making gravy and add a couple big spoonfuls of the confit garlic cloves. Fry for 30 seconds before deglazing with the vegetable stock, making sure to scrape up all the yummy cooked-on bits. Pour the jus all over the cauliflower and spoon over the tahini dressing. Dust with paprika and finish with a ton of fresh parsley and the leftover half lemon, cut into wedges.

Even though this dish is vegan, somewhat by accident we've found it goes really well with grilled steaks.

MONSTER ISLAND COCKTAIL

This cocktail contains three strong flavors from famous islands and is garnished with a flamed orange peel. The Peat Monster whiskey is a homage to Godzilla and his island hometown of Tokyo.

MAKES 1 DRINK

1½ ounces Peat Monster scotch whiskey
1 ounce Averna Amaro Siciliano
2 dashes Angostura bitters
Orange peel

Combine first three ingredients in a mixing glass. Add ice, stir, and strain into a chilled cocktail glass. Garnish with a flamed orange peel.

Rosa Mexicano

575 7th Street NW
Washington, DC 20004
(202) 783-5522
ROSAMEXICANO.COM
Executive Regional Chef: Steven Lukis

Josefina Howard was ahead of the times. Back in 1984, when most people thought farm-to-table to be a string of words thrown together, the Rosa Mexicano founder insisted that the guacamole at her upscale Mexican restaurant be made tableside. Howard wanted her guests to see the caliber and freshness of the ingredients being used in what has become a signature dish for the restaurant that now claims many locations beyond that first one in New York City.

Creating a paste from the onions, cilantro, lime, and jalapeños, stands as the first and really the key step in crafting the guacamole. "The proof is in the paste," says the restaurant's Executive Regional Chef Steven Lukis, who is one of the people charged with training staff in the art of making the popular avocado dip that comes served with house-made corn tortilla chips. "The paste is the secret to the guacamole."

Everyone who works at Rosa Mexicano must go through something of a guacamole boot camp, spending hour after hour, day after day, perfecting the technique needed to create the tableside dish. Special attention is paid to making the perfect paste and the technique of folding in the ingredients layer by later. Diners get to choose from three degrees of spice when they start their meal with the guacamole, and the staff learns to deliver the right amount of heat into each made-to-order batch. If you want to attempt the recipe at home, Lukis strongly recommends investing in a *molcajete,* a Mexican mortar and pestle carved from volcanic rock, an invention that dates back thousands of years and was used by both the Aztecs and Mayans.

Guacamole en Molcajete

SERVES 4

For chili paste:

1 tablespoon finely chopped white onion
1 tablespoon chopped fresh cilantro
2 teaspoons finely chopped jalapeño, or more to taste
1 teaspoon salt, or as needed

3 medium-ripe but firm Hass avocados
3 tablespoons diced plum tomato
2 tablespoons chopped fresh cilantro
1 tablespoon finely chopped white onion
Salt if necessary

Special equipment: Molcajete

To prepare the chili paste: Grind the onion, cilantro, jalapeño, and salt together in a molcajete until all the ingredients are very finely ground. Alternatively, use a fork to mash all the ingredients to a paste in a wide hardwood bowl.

To assemble: Cut each avocado in half, working the knife blade around the pit. Twist the halves to separate them and flick out the pit with the tip of the knife. Fold a kitchen towel in quarters and

hold it in the palm of your "non-knife" hand. Rest an avocado half, cut-side up, in your palm and make three or four evenly spaced lengthwise cuts through the avocado flesh, without cutting through the skin. Make four crosswise cuts in the same way. Scoop the diced avocado flesh into the molcajete. Repeat with the remaining avocado halves.

Gently fold the avocado into the paste, keeping the avocado in as large pieces as possible. Add the tomato, cilantro, and onion and fold in gently. Taste and add salt if necessary. Serve immediately, right from the molcajete or bowl, with chips and tortillas.

Soupergirl

314 Carroll Street NW
Washington, DC 20012
(202) 609-7177
THESOUPERGIRL.COM
Chef/Owner: Sara Polon

What's the difference between a stand-up comedian and a vegetarian soup entrepreneur? I have no idea but chances are Sara Polon does. In fact, I bet the comic turned soup seller could nail that set up's punch line while at the same time whipping up a batch of gazpacho and stirring a steamy pot of mulligatawny stew. No word yet on whether she could do it while standing on one foot or with a hand tied behind her back, but my hunch is that she could. After all, they don't call her Soupergirl for nothing.

Washington-area native Polon made the unlikely leap from comic to soup cook following a four-year stint playing the New York City club circuit by night and working government contracts during day. Eventually, she tired of the grind and came back to DC to figure out what came next. A life-changing read of Michael Pollan's book *The Omnivore's Dilemma* provided the answer. Polon decided to join the local food movement and soon thereafter landed on the idea of starting an organic, vegan soup business that only used locally sourced and in-season ingredients. The only missing piece was pulling her mom aka Marilyn Polon aka Soupermom aka the best soup-maker around out of retirement. "So now she's allowed to say that I need a haircut or that she hates my shoes because I brought her out of retirement," Sara says.

The pair cook together every week, cooking up soups for the subscription service and the shop where you can eat in or take out that week's soups. Marilyn came up with the secret to the West African Peanut Stew—lots of peanut butter and cutting the sweet potatoes into big pieces before cooking them together for a long, long time until they melt.

"It's really rich, people just go crazy for it," says Sara adding that the first time they made the soup, which has turned into their best-seller, they were convinced it was going to bomb. "Now we always sell out. We have to brace staff when we put it on the menu."

Giving the audience what it wants, be it new material or West African Peanut Stew, is the similarity between stand-up comedian and a vegetarian soup entrepreneur. "At the end of the day the audience, or the customer, decides if you are a hit or a miss," she says. Thank you, Sara. We are glad that you and your soup will be here all week.

WEST AFRICAN PEANUT STEW

MAKES ABOUT 11 CUPS

2 teaspoons canola oil

2 cups roughly chopped onion

1 tablespoon freshly ground cumin (toast the seeds and then grind them)

1 cup roasted peanuts, or ¾ to 1 cup of store-bought peanut butter (you can add more to taste)

6 cups peeled, cubed sweet potato (approximately 1-inch dice, large enough for the sweet potatoes to melt into the soup)

2 (15-ounce) cans chickpeas, drained

1 (28-ounce) can diced tomatoes

3½ cups vegetable broth (homemade please!)

½ teaspoon black pepper

¼ teaspoon salt

To begin the soup, heat oil in a stockpot over a medium-high heat. Sauté onions until very soft. Add the cumin and cook for another minute. Don't burn your spice!

Put peanuts in a blender and process to a paste. Add peanut butter, sweet potato, chickpeas, tomatoes, and broth to the pot. (If using commercial peanut butter, choose an all-natural brand—don't use Jif. Don't be afraid to use more as well—people love peanut butter!) Bring to a boil.

Reduce heat and simmer, uncovered, for 30 minutes, until the potatoes are soft—they should melt into the soup, which gives it a nice, natural sweetness.

Stir often to avoid burning! The soup is heavy and the ingredients can fall to the bottom of the pot and burn!

Season to taste—the seasoning listed above is just a guideline. If you make your own peanut butter, you might need a bit more salt.

Add more peanut butter if needed.

THE SOURCE
BY WOLFGANG PUCK

575 PENNSYLVANIA AVENUE NW
WASHINGTON, DC 20565
(202) 637-6100
WOLFGANGPUCK.COM/RESTAURANTS
EXECUTIVE CHEF: SCOTT DREWNO

When Scott Drewno turned twenty-one, he left home, moved to Las Vegas, and fell in love. But Drewno's tale is not one of a quickie-wedding-chapel-Elvis-impersonator-what-happens-in-Vegas-stays-in-Vegas cliché. Instead Scott's story starts in the kitchen of Chinois, Wolfgang Puck's decidedly Elvis impersonator–free Asian fusion restaurant, where Scott worked as line cook, found a mentor, and discovered a whole new world of flavors he never knew about in the small upstate New York town where he grew up.

"I was taken aback and amazed by things like ginger and lemongrass and cooking with a wok and whole roasted duck," tells the soft-spoken executive chef of The Source, housed in the magnificent Newseum. "I fell in love."

Fast-forward some 20 years later and Drewno's love affair with Asian cuisine and techniques is still going strong. From his kitchen at The Source, the chef creates traditional Asian dishes with a modern, upscale flair. The chef's commitment to locally sourced ingredients also comes through in all of his dishes, including this one for Velvet Corn Soup.

Drewno based this recipe on a traditional velvet corn soup he tasted on one of his many trips to China. The luxurious mouthfeel of the dish won him over. The warm, creamy soup only appears on the menu during corn season, much to the dismay of its many fans. The good news is that other seasonally driven soups, like his spring pea, take its place when corn season comes to a close. For those who prefer a non-chicken stock, Drewno recommends creating a simple corn stock, as he often does. He recommends cooking corncobs, celery, onion, and carrots together, and then letting the stock simmer for an hour or two. Wearing your blue suede shoes as your stir also doesn't hurt.

Velvet Corn Soup with Maryland Jumbo Lump Crab & Chili Oil

MAKES 1½ QUARTS

15 ears corn
1 small white onion
¼ pound butter
Sea salt and pepper, to taste
2 cups chicken stock
1 quart heavy cream
2 ounces per serving of Maryland jumbo lump crabmeat
Chili oil to taste
1 tablespoon chopped scallions

Grate corn on a box grater with large holes. Sweat out onions with butter over low heat. Add grated corn and sweat out. Season to taste with salt and pepper. Place stock and cream in a pot and bring to a boil, and then add hot cream and hot chicken stock to corn and onion mixture and simmer.

Adjust seasoning. Puree in blender and pass through a sieve.

Serve with crabmeat and garnish with chili oil and scallions.

STICKY FINGERS BAKERY

1370 PARK ROAD NW
WASHINGTON, DC 20010
(202) 299-9700
STICKYFINGERSBAKERY.COM
OWNER: DORON PETERSAN; HEAD BAKER: JENNY WEBB; SPECIALTY
CAKE DECORATOR AND GUM PASTE DESIGNER: KAMBER SHERROD;
PASTRY CHEF: RAMON OSORIO; PRODUCTION BAKER: KEVIN KALB

With cupcakes and kindness, Doron Petersan kills the notion that you can't make to-die-for baked goods without eggs and butter. Petersan, along with Sticky Fingers Bakery head baker Jenny Webb, beat out the conventional competition not once but twice for the win on the popular Food Network's *Cupcake Wars,* and awards dot the walls and website of the aqua and pink shop with its funky vintage diner–style vibe and neighborhood hangout feel. Even with all the titles and praise, it's the taste of the cookies, cakes, brownies, and other sweet treats sold at the vegan bakery that keep people coming back for more.

"If it didn't taste good, we wouldn't be here," says Petersan, the Sticky Fingers owner who is as delightful as the baked goods housed behind the counter of her Columbia Heights shop. File Petersan's bakery ownership under "necessity is the mother of

invention." The native New Yorker started the dairy- and egg-free bakery in 2002 after taking the vegan plunge and not being able to find any yummy vegan desserts here in her new hometown of DC. She began the bakery in a small space on 18th Street with a business partner who left under good terms in 2009 to move to California to join an Iron Maiden tribute band. (File that under "happens all the time in the vegan bakery world.") "We started the place with a $20,000 loan, a very ambitious business plan, and a stupid amount of confidence," she laughs.

The unlikely approach paid off. In 2006, she opened the current spot and expanded the business to include savories and a sit-down area. Although she can whip up a sticky bun with the best of them, Petersan makes no bones, no pun intended, about her role.

"I'm not a pastry chef," she says. "I'm a business owner. I clean the bathroom and sign paychecks and run day-to-day errands. I go to Whole Foods and Home Depot. Most of what I do is say yes, no, good idea, or maybe try this."

Still, despite her downplaying her baking role, it's clear Petersan possesses quite a bit of her own kitchen wisdom. Before starting the business, the avid cyclist and mother of a young son studied food science and nutrition and worked as a baker and bartender. She attributes the leave-them-wanting-more taste of her baked goods to the techniques they use at the shop to create flavors rather than simply throwing in substitutions. "It's the way we incorporate the ingredients and mix them together that makes it work," she says.

Her love of simple yet delicious flavors like the ones she uses in this recipe she attributes to her family, and growing up in her family's strong Jewish and Italian (or Jewtalian, as she calls it) food culture.

WHY, OH WHY?

If Doron Petersan had a nickel for every time she gets asked the why'd-you-go-vegan question, she would, well, she'd have an awful lot of nickels. I couldn't resist putting my five cents in and asking the question too. Here is what I found out. The Sticky Fingers owner was twenty-two and working as a vet assistant when she had her first no-more-meat moment. One day while helping with a surgery, she made the connection between the food on her plate and the animal on the table and then and there decided to change her diet. That is until she had one more hurrah. "I stood over my grandmother's sink and ate everything I could get my hands on—meatballs, chicken cutlets, everything."

Blooming Cherry Blossom Cupcakes

VANILLA CUPCAKE, TART CHERRY FILLING, ALMOND CRÈME
FROSTING, AND TOASTED ALMONDS

MAKES 18 CUPCAKES OR 2 9-INCH ROUND CAKES

3 cups (11½ ounces) all-purpose flour

1 tablespoon baking powder

½ teaspoon salt

1⅓ cups (8⁸⁄₁₀ ounces) sugar

½ (4 ounces) cup non-hydrogenated vegan margarine
(Earth Balance brand recommended)

½ cup water

1½ teaspoons egg replacer (Ener-G brand
recommended)

¾ cup soy milk

2 teaspoons vanilla extract

Preheat the oven to 350°F. Line two 9-inch round
cake pans with parchment or place liners in
cupcake trays.

Sift the flour, baking powder, and salt into a
medium-size bowl. Set the bowl aside.

In the bowl of an electric stand mixer, cream
the sugar and the margarine with the whisk
attachment, about 5 minutes. Scrape down the
sides and bottom of the bowl.

In a small bowl or cup, combine the water and
egg replacer and stir to dissolve the egg replacer.
Add the egg replacer to the sugar and mix until
combined.

In a small bowl, combine the soy milk and vanilla
and set aside.

Turn the mixer speed to low and slowly add the
dry ingredients and the soy milk, alternating
between the two, ending with the soy milk.

Fill lined cupcake tin ¾ full and bake for 16–19
minutes, or until toothpick inserted in the center
comes out clean.

Cherry Filling

MAKES ABOUT 2 CUPS

2 cups pitted cherries, fresh or frozen, pureed

1 tablespoon lemon juice

1 cup sugar

¼ cup water

¼ cup cornstarch

In a medium, heavy-bottom saucepot, stir
together the cherries, lemon juice, and sugar.

Heat on medium-high until the mixture begins to
bubble around the edges.

In a small bowl, mix the water and cornstarch into
a slurry.

Slowly add the cornstarch mixture to the cherries
while whisking. Cook for 2 more minutes while
stirring until it becomes pourable. Let cool
completely.

FROSTING

MAKES ENOUGH FROSTING TO FROST A 2-LAYER
9-INCH CAKE OR 18 CUPCAKES

1 cup plus 2 tablespoons nonhydrogenated
   vegetable shortening (Earth Balance brand
   recommended)
¼ cup plus 2 tablespoons nonhydrogenated
   vegan margarine (Earth Balance brand
   recommended)
4½ cups 10x powdered sugar
3½ teaspoons vanilla extract
2 teaspoons almond extract
2 to 4 tablespoons soy milk, as needed
½ cup almond slices

In the bowl of a stand mixer, whip shortening
and margarine with the paddle attachment until
completely combined. Scrape the bottom of
the bowl to ensure that all ingredients are mixed
thoroughly.

On low speed, slowly add sugar a little at a time.

Once the sugar is incorporated, add the
vanilla and almond extracts and soy milk, one
tablespoon at a time, and mix on low until the
liquids are incorporated.

Scrape the bottom of the bowl and mix on
medium-high speed until all ingredients are
combined and frosting is fluffy, about 2 minutes.

Spread almonds on a baking sheet and bake for
10–15 minutes at 350°F. Let cool.

Assembly: Once cupcakes are cooled, using a
paring knife or a frosting tip, poke a hole in the top
center of the cupcake about ½ inch down into
the middle. With a spoon or a pastry bag fill the
hole with cherry filling, about 1 tablespoon. Frost
your cupcake using a piping bag or spatula. Tip
your cupcake and roll the frosting in the toasted
almonds and coat as desired. Enjoy!

Sunflower Bakery

8507 Ziggy Lane
Gaithersburg, MD 20877
(240) 361-3698
SUNFLOWERBAKERY.ORG
Executive Pastry Chef: Elizabeth Hutter

Every morning it's back to school for Chef Elizabeth Hutter. The former Watergate Hotel pastry chef dons her apron and heads to the front of her industrial-kitchen-slash-classroom to teach the ins and outs of professional baking to her students, adults with development and other disabilities. But her lessons are not just a dry run. The Sunflower Bakery is a true working kitchen where the students fill customer orders each day with the delicious cookies, cakes, and other treats they bake as part of the nonprofit organization's on-the-job training program.

"We don't adapt the bakery to them," tells Hutter. "We plan our day based on the orders. The students are getting real job experience."

The experience proves to be invaluable. Sunflower graduates go on to get baking jobs at places like Safeway, Bundles of Cookies, and Stella's Bakery, where they put into action the skills they have learned from Hutter and the Sunflower team. "We train people to get out and work at other sites," she shares.

The Gaithersburg-based program runs a popular "sweets of the month" subscription program. You can either pick up your goodies at the bakery or at pre-designated drop-off locations around town. The program is particularly popular at, but by no means limited to, Jewish schools and synagogues as Sunflower is also a certified kosher bakery. As a result, all the items that come out of the kitchen are pareve, which means they contain no meat or dairy ingredients, including butter. The laws of keeping kosher dictate a strict separation between meat and any food containing milk products hence the need for neutral or pareve desserts that can be eaten in the same meal with either. Despite its kosher status, Sunflower is a nonsectarian organization and is open to students of all religions. Hutter, who herself is not Jewish, did a quick prep on substitutions and kosher laws before taking over the kitchen and adapts all the recipes they use to fit the standards as she did with this mandel bread. "Our mandel bread is really good, it's like a biscotti but not as hard," she says. "Margarine doesn't get as hard as butter so when you sub margarine in for butter, you wind up with a cookie that is going to be a bit more chewy. Ideally you should cut up your margarine like ice cubes and put it in the freezer for a half hour before using it. That way it's more like butter."

COMBO MANDEL BREAD

MAKES ABOUT 8 DOZEN PIECES

2¼ cups (12 ounces) all-purpose flour

1 cup (8 ounces) granulated sugar

1½ teaspoons baking powder

Pinch of salt

6 ounces cold salted margarine*

5 ounces dried cranberries

9 ounces semisweet chocolate chunks/chips

6 ounces slivered almonds (not sliced)

3 large eggs

1 teaspoon vanilla extract

*Margarine breaks down faster than butter, so you really have to keep the margarine cold. Put it in the freezer for half an hour before using and it will be more like butter.

Preheat the oven to 325°F. Line two half-sheet pans with parchment paper.

Combine the flour, sugar, baking powder, and salt in a 5-quart mixing bowl and mix well on low speed, using a paddle attachment.

Cut cold margarine into small pieces and toss into the mixing bowl. Mix on low speed until the margarine is incorporated and the mixture is cool and powdery.

Pour in the fruit, chocolate, and nuts, mixing briefly to combine.

Whisk the eggs and vanilla together in a small bowl.

Beat in the eggs and vanilla to the margarine/flour mix on low speed, taking time to scrape the bottom of the bowl very well.

Turn the dough out onto a floured surface and knead it lightly, making sure that the fruit, nuts, and chocolate are evenly distributed. Divide the dough into four equal pieces, each weighing about 13 ounces.

Roll each piece of dough into a smooth log about 12 inches long on a lightly floured board.

Place the logs on sheet pans lengthwise, spacing them 4 inches apart. Bake for 35–40 minutes or until the logs are golden and firm to the touch.

Remove pan from oven. Allow the logs to cool completely. (After they cool, they may be wrapped and frozen for finishing at a later date.)

Carefully place the cooled logs on a cutting board. Use a serrated knife to carefully cut the mandel into half-inch-thick slices. Arrange the cookies on the baking sheets, laying them flat.

Bake for a second time at 325°F until the mandel are golden, about 10–15 minutes. Cool the mandel completely before wrapping in airtight container.

Store cookies at room temperature for up to 5 days or freeze for up to 3 months.

Tabard Inn

1739 N Street NW
Washington, DC 20036
(202) 331-8528
TABARDINN.COM/RESTAURANT
Executive Chef: Paul Pelt
Pastry Chef: Huw Griffiths

Memories at the Tabard Inn Restaurant are an off-menu item, but someone always seems to be ordering them up at the restaurant at the historic Dupont Circle hotel.

The staff reports hearing stories of people who dined or stayed at the eclectic forty-room inn, which is made up of three brick row houses. Recently a man who came in for dinner told a story of how he stayed at the Tabard Inn in 1974 when he was thirteen years old and how he vividly remembers gray and teal tiles on the floor. A little sleuth work in the office uncovered photos that unearthed a picture confirming his recollection.

The memories also extend behind the scenes of the restaurant. In the pastry section of the kitchen, a photo of a woman named Frances is affixed to the refrigerator door, watching over the busy chefs as they roll dough and plate desserts. Frances began her decades-long career at the Tabard Inn as a breakfast line cook in the late 1970s. Over the years she worked in several different departments until she retired not too long ago from accounts payable. Her picture, no doubt a caring tribute to a longtime colleague, stands as yet another literal and figurative snapshot of the Tabard Inn story.

Those coming in these days to make their own memories may want to opt for the coveted patio seating. The outdoor courtyard is dotted with art and found objects placed there by the Tabard Inn's on-staff curator, who has an eagle eye for the different and unusual. When it comes to art, menu, and memory at this N Street gem, you just never know exactly what you are going to find.

HOUSING WAVES

During World War II, the Tabard Inn served as a boarding-house for seventy women from the Navy Women Accepted for Volunteer Emergency Service (WAVES), the nickname for an all-woman division of the US Navy formed during that war. The inn, first opened as a guesthouse in 1922, provided housing for these women serving their country for two years, from 1943 to 1945. WAVE Luella Moenter worked as a Cook 2nd Class in the Tabard Inn kitchen during those years and recently celebrated her ninety-fifth birthday with well wishes from the Tabard Inn staff.

POACHED EGGS WITH WILD MUSHROOM & ANCHO CHILI SALSA

MAKES 8 SERVINGS

For the ancho chili salsa:

3 tablespoons olive oil
½ cup wild mushrooms
1 shallot, diced
1 tablespoon epazote
Salt and pepper
2 ancho chilis
1 cup water
2 poblano chilis
4 plum tomatoes
4 cloves garlic
½ teaspoon salt

8 corn tortillas
8 eggs

For the refried beans:

2 cups dried black beans (you can also use pintos
  or another favorite bean)
6 cups chicken stock
1 tablespoon salt
1 yellow onion
1 jalapeño
4 garlic cloves
½ cup lard (or ¼ cup bacon fat and ¼ cup olive oil)
1 teaspoon ground cumin

To prepare the ancho chili salsa: Heat 3 table-spoons of olive oil in a pan. Sauté your favorite wild mushrooms for 2–3 minutes, along with shallot, epazote, and a pinch of salt and pepper.

Toast dried ancho chilis in the oven for 3 minutes at 300°F. Remove from the oven, remove the seeds, and then soak the chilis in ½ cup water. Once they are soft (this takes about 20 minutes), julienne the chilis and set them aside.

Rub poblano chilis with olive oil and roast them in the oven at 350°F, 10–15 minutes or until skins blister (or over a burner on the stove if you prefer). Cool the poblanos, peel them, and remove the seeds.

Roast plum tomatoes with cloves of garlic at 350°F for 20–30 minutes until the tomatoes are soft.

Place the roasted tomatoes and garlic and the ancho chilis in a blender or food processor with salt and ½ cup of water. Pulse only until coarsely chopped. Pour the mixture in a bowl and add the mushrooms and poblano chilis.

To prepare the refried beans: Soak the beans overnight. After the beans have been soaked, discard water. Take the soaked beans and simmer them in chicken stock and salt for about one hour until the beans are tender. Check that the beans are tender.

In a separate pan, roast 1 thickly sliced yellow onion, 1 jalapeño pepper, and peeled garlic. When the beans are tender, place them in a food processor with the onion, jalapeno, and garlic. Puree until smooth.

Refry the beans in lard (or a mixture of olive oil and bacon fat) and 1 teaspoon of ground cumin for 5–10 minutes, until it develops the consistency of thick paste.

Fry the corn tortillas in the same fat used for the beans until brown/crisp on both sides and poach the eggs.

To serve: Spread the refried beans on each tortilla and top with a poached egg and the chili salsa.

Sticky Toffee Pecan Pudding Cake

MAKES 10 8-OUNCE RAMEKINS

12 ounces chopped dates

1½ cups boiling water

2 tablespoons vanilla extract

1½ teaspoons baking soda

6 ounces unsalted butter, room temperature

10 ounces granulated sugar

4 eggs, room temperature

2½ cups all-purpose flour

4 teaspoons baking powder

Pinch salt

For toffee sauce:

12 ounces brown sugar

8 ounces butter, unsalted

6 ounces heavy cream

10 ounces toasted pecan pieces

Special equipment: Ice cream machine

Preheat oven to 325°F. Combine dates, water, vanilla extract, and baking soda and let sit for 30 minutes.

Beat the butter and sugar in a mixer with paddle attachment until light and fluffy. Gradually (one at a time) add eggs and scrape bowl well.

Sift flour, baking powder, and salt. In two additions, add dates and flour. Scrape bowl and paddle well, until well incorporated

Coat 10 ramekins with nonstick cooking spray.

With a 3-ounce ice cream scoop, transfer batter to ramekins.

Bake 15–20 minutes or until middle bounces back when touched. Remove from oven and cool for 15 minutes.

To prepare toffee sauce: In a heavy-bottom pot, stir brown sugar, butter, and heavy cream over low heat until the sugar dissolves. Unmold cooled pudding cakes. Ladle ¼ cup of toffee sauce and a small handful of pecans into each ramekin. Place pudding cakes back into toffee-sauced ramekins.

Before serving, return to oven (325°F) for 5 minutes.

To serve: Invert ramekin to serving plate to release pudding cake.

Nutella Gelato

1¼ cups granulated sugar

1¼ cups water

1 vanilla bean, split

8 ounces Nutella

To prepare the gelato, boil sugar, water and vanilla. Remove bean pod.

Let cool until cold.

Combine the Nutella and simple syrup in blender until smooth. Churn in an ice cream machine.

Table

903 N Street NW
Washington, DC 20001
(202) 288-1824
TABLEDC.COM
Chef/Owner: Frederik De Pue

And now for something entirely different. A sweet little European-style eatery with no menus, no reservations, no cocktail list, and no rush to turn over tables. The offerings are cooked based on what the chef purchased that day and you can pop in for breakfast, lunch, or dinner and stay as long as you like on your laptop, sipping a glass of wine, or chasing a daydream. The vibe at the Shaw spot, just a construction site when we visited it, is old school meets urban. The food, homey yet unconventional. Its name, Table, is pronounced the French way, "tawb-luh."

"It's something I have had in mind for the longest time," says Chef/Owner Frederik De Pue, who was born and raised in Belgium. "A restaurant where you don't work with a set menu. Where it feels like you are walking into a home and see what is cooking tonight."

De Pue first made Washington, DC, his home in 2001 when he came here to be the executive chef to the European Commission Delegation Ambassador. After several years De Pue moved beyond embassy circles and began his catering company 42° Catering, named after the forty-second parallel, which connects many of the greatest gastronomic cities of the world.

Through his private catering and now at Table, housed in a former two-story garage, the chef will use some proteins not often found at restaurants here in town, like frogs' legs (an ingredient, he says, that is easily purchased at most Asian markets). "People enjoy the dish tremendously," he says. "When I've made them before, people were practically licking the plate. Sometimes you have to go for it."

PAN-ROASTED FROGS' LEGS WITH
SORREL CREAM & FINGERLING POTATOES

SERVES 4

12 large fingerling potatoes

2 pounds fresh frogs' legs

3 small shallots

3 bunches of sorrel

2 cloves of garlic, peeled

2 tablespoons unsalted butter

Salt and pepper, to taste

1 cup Chardonnay or other dry white wine

1 cup heavy cream

Start by placing the fingerling potatoes in salted water and bring to a boil until they are fully cooked.

Place them in ice water to stop the cooking process and peel them thoroughly and set aside. Wash the frogs' legs and dry completely on a paper towel, dabbing to remove all surface moisture.

Thinly slice the shallots and chop the sorrel. Peel the garlic and roughly chop, press a palm on the flat of a large chef's knife and then smash the garlic down until finely minced/pureed. Cut the frogs' legs in half. In large skillet melt the butter and cook down to create brown butter.

Season the frogs' legs with salt and pepper and place them carefully in the pan. Give the frogs' legs the time to sauté for about 2–3 minutes. Turn over, add the shallots, and let all cook for about 2 minutes. Add the sorrel and garlic.

Once all vegetables are fully cooked, add the white wine and reduce by half, then add the heavy cream and reduce again by half. Finish seasoning with salt and pepper and serve with fingerling potatoes on the side.

Rabbit Tenderloin, Pomme Maxim with Radish Salad, Grilled Scallions & Jus d'Orval

SERVES 4

1 carrot

2 shallots

2 cloves garlic

2 whole rabbits, butchered (remaining bones and other parts should be saved for stock)

½ tablespoon of sesame oil

¼ cup olive oil

1 bay leaf

2 sprigs of thyme

1 (12 ounce) bottle Orval beer

2 cups veal stock

4 large Yukon Gold potatoes

12 sage leaves

16 radishes

½ tablespoon fresh lime juice

Salt and pepper, to taste

12 scallions

Peel the carrot, shallots, and garlic cloves and chop all very finely, brunoise-style. In large skillet, sear the rabbit bones with some of the sesame oil and a bit of olive oil until dark brown. Add the chopped vegetables, bay leaf, and thyme with a bit more oil. After cooking down for 5 minutes, deglaze the pan with the Orval beer, bringing all to a boil. Reduce the entire amount by ⅔, add the veal stock and let simmer for about 2½ hours. Remove the sauce and reserve until serving.

Wash and peel the potatoes, dry, and slice into rounds using a mandoline. Slice approximately 20 pieces per serving. Place potato slices in small stacks of five pieces each, in a hot pan with some olive oil. Season with salt and pepper and bake at 350°F until golden brown. Remove, set aside, and keep warm.

Season the rabbit legs and add to an ovenproof pan with some olive oil over medium heat. Sear until golden brown. Add the shoulders and place pan in the oven with half of the sage for about 15 minutes, roasting at 350°F. Remove from the oven and move to the stovetop. Add the tenderloin, and cook covered, over medium heat with some sage until fully cooked, or about 4 minutes.

Assemble the plate with rabbit pieces, and add three potato stacks to each plate. Drizzle the rabbit with the sauce. Julienne the radishes and toss with the remaining sesame oil, lime juice, and salt and add to the plate. Grill or sear the scallions and add to the plate as final garnish.

Taylor Gourmet

1116 H Street NE
Washington, DC 20002
(202) 684-7001
TAYLORGOURMET.COM
Co-Owners: Casey Patten and David Mazza

One day Casey Patten spent a lunch hour in the conference room at his first post-college job outlining this little idea he had to open a sub shop in DC. His plan filled up the entire whiteboard and the scribbles were soon after erased. Patten had even forgotten about that day until recently when a friend reminded him of his white board pipedream. What he has recalled all along was wanting to bring good sub sandwiches to the nation's capital from the moment he moved to town.

"I grew up in Philadelphia and back home you can get a good hoagie readily on almost any corner," says Patten, the co-owner of Taylor Gourmet, which started on H Street and now has several locations in DC, suburban Maryland, and Northern Virginia. "Then I ended up in DC and went looking for a really good hoagie—I heard you called them a sandwich or sub here—and couldn't find one anywhere. I spent years and years looking."

He did the only logical thing to stop his wondering—he opened his own sandwich place. Along with his business partner David Mazza, they created the neighborhood shop that Patten had been so persistently looking for around every DC corner.

Patten and Mazza, who have known each other since their teenage years in Philly, pride themselves on making most everything in house and using high-quality ingredients that go beyond what one typically finds at the corner store. All the sauces and dressings

are created in house, the roast beef is made every day, and the veggies are sliced several times a day so they are always fresh. The bread is the only piece of the sandwich puzzle not sourced at the shop. For that, Taylor Gourmet contracts out with a friend who makes the rolls that hold the meats, cheeses, and other fillings. When making the recipe at home, Patten recommends using a rustic ciabatta bread or even a seeded Italian loaf—just make sure to scoop the inside out a little bit, he suggests, before loading on the roast beef, brie, and other toppings.

12" Cherry Street Hoagie

MAKES 1 HOAGIE

*Roast Beef (yields 7–9 lbs cooked weight or
    20 3.5-ounce portions)*

4–5 pounds average eye of round roast
10 whole garlic cloves
¼ cup salt
2½ tablespoons black pepper
2½ tablespoons red pepper
2 tablespoons olive pomace oil

Cherry Pepper Garlic Sauce (makes 2 quarts of sauce)

1¼ cup cherry peppers, minced
2 cups roasted garlic
2 tablespoons salt
3 cups cherry pepper brine
1 cup oil

Your favorite 12-inch hoagie rolls (in the store we use
    our traditional old world Italian loaf)
2 ounces cherry pepper garlic sauce
6 ounces (2 portions) roast beef
3 slices of brie
1.5 ounces arugula
6 shakes Italian seasoning
½ ounce (1 pass) oil

To prepare the roast beef: Start by pre-heating your oven to 350°F. Remove the meat from the plastic and wash off excess blood.

Place roast on a cutting board and make 10 cuts into the beef. Cuts in the beef should be randomly placed being sure that the entire roast beef is being cut. Cuts should be deep enough and wide enough to fit garlic cloves.

In a separate pan, mix salt, black pepper, and red pepper together being sure to mix thoroughly.

Place the 10 garlic cloves in the cuts made in the meat.

Take 2 tablespoons of the pomace oil and massage it into the entire piece of meat. Take the spice rub and rub the entire piece of meat being sure to get the spices into the cuts in the meat and on the bottom side of the roast.

Place the roast beef on a sheet tray fat side up and slide the tray into an oven that has been pre-heated to 350°F.

Place thermometer half way into the thickest part of the beef and set it for 120°F. When the thermometer goes off, remove roast beef from the oven and place on a cooling rack for one hour.

After the meat has cooled for an hour, remove the roast beef from the pan and wrap thoroughly in plastic.

Place a piece of masking tape with the date on the plastic and refrigerate at 41°F or below for up to two days.

To prepare the cherry pepper garlic sauce: Place a clean cutting board and food processor on a prep table or counter.

Take the cherry peppers out of the refrigerator and set aside 20 peppers.

Remove the stems from the cherry peppers and place in the food processor. Turn on the food processor and blend until cherry peppers are ¼" inch in size.

Remove the cherry peppers from food processor and set aside.

Place 2 cups of roasted garlic and 1 cup of oil in the food processor and blend until the roasted garlic is pureed and creamy. Add 2 tablespoons of salt, 1¼ cups of minced cherry peppers, and 3 cups of cherry pepper brine to the food processor and mix all the ingredients thoroughly. The cherry pepper pieces should be noticeable in the sauce.

Turn the food processor on and slowly drizzle in 1 cup of oil to emulsify the sauce, taking special care to make sure the oil is poured in slowly.

Using a funnel, pour finished cherry pepper sauce into a 32-ounce squeeze bottle.

Label, date, and refrigerate the sauce.

To assemble the hoagie: Open up a 12" hoagie roll. Spread cherry pepper garlic sauce to the bottom of the hoagie roll. Fluff and evenly spread roast beef across the entire bottom of the hoagie roll. Place brie cheese lengthwise across the top of the roast beef. (If brie cheese slices are small 4 slices may be needed.) Place arugula on top of the brie cheese and spread evenly across entire hoagie.

On top of the greens shake Italian seasoning across entire hoagie. Add oil across entire hoagie. Close hoagie roll, using bread knife to hold all of the ingredients inside the sandwich. Slice hoagie diagonally into two equal halves. To avoid injury, place fingers and thumb on the side of the hoagie to allow knife to be drawn through the sandwich freely. Extra meat and extra cheese can be added if you want an even thicker hoagie.

Note: Hoagie should always be built of the flat part of the hoagie roll. This is considered the bottom of the roll.

Teaism

2009 R Street NW
Washington, DC 20009
(202) 667-3827
teaism.com
Co-Owners: Linda Neuman and Michelle Brown
Chef: Allison Swope

Linda Neuman, Michelle Brown, and Allison Swope met back in the days of shoulder pads at the Executive Club, a membership club for local professional women. Michelle managed the restaurant, Alison was the chef, and Linda worked in the restaurant at the Dupont Circle club, which had a workout room and a restaurant. It was the summer of 1984. "That was when the restaurant industry seduced me away from my degree in economics," says Linda, who was a Georgetown student at the time.

Later on, the three women worked together at Michelle's restaurant New Heights, and now, more than 25 years later, the trio is happily reunited at Teaism, the teahouse Michelle and Linda opened in 1996. The three women run the charming teahouse, examining everything that comes into the kitchen to make sure it is whole, organic, and unprocessed. "Allison and Michelle are so rigorous about scrutinizing our ingredients, making sure nothing has trans fats, high fructose corn syrups, additives, or is genetically modified," Neuman says.

The countries where tea comes from serve as the inspiration for the menu. "People tend to think Britain when they think tea, but tea doesn't grow in England," Neuman points outs. "It grows in places like China, Vietnam, Japan, and India."

The Teaism team approaches its tea offerings much like a wine list, refining and tasting the selections all the time for color, clarity, and brew. "Tea, like wine, is an agricultural product," she explains.

SEW YOUR SALTY OATS

The Salty Oat Cookies sold at Teaism are the kind of cookies legends are made of. Online, loyal fans of the thick, chewy, raisin-filled cookie hypothesize about the well-guarded recipe and many a post has been devoted to broadcasting praises of the iconic treat.

Terri Horn, a former Washingtonian who worked as a pastry chef at places like Marvelous Market and 1789, is the mastermind behind the cookie. She developed the recipe over several years and when Teaism opened, she allowed the store to sell the salt-dotted creations. The shop, which keeps a backup ingredients list in case the items on the Horn-approved list are not in stock, jumped at the chance. Teaism pays Horn, who now lives in Maine and owns Kayak Cookie, a royalty for each and every salty oat cookie sold. Four times a year Horn goes down to DC to do quality-control checks and make sure the cookie is holding true to her well-guarded recipe. "We sold 158,000 last year or about 13,000 a month," says Neuman. With those kinds of sales, it's no wonder the Teaism team is contractually obligated to keep the recipe a secret.

BUCKWHEAT & HEMP HEART PANCAKES

YIELDS APPROXIMATELY 10 5-INCH PANCAKES

For apple compote:

6 Granny Smith apples, peeled, cored,
    cut into 8 wedges each
½ cup brown sugar
1 teaspoon cinnamon

For pancakes:

1½ cups buckwheat flour
1½ cups pastry flour
1 tablespoon baking powder
1 teaspoon baking soda
½ teaspoon salt
2 cups buttermilk
4 eggs
1½ cups milk
2 tablespoons honey
¼ cup rice bran oil
1 cup hemp seeds
Dried cranberries
Maple syrup

To prepare the compote: Place all ingredients in small sauté pan over medium heat.

Stir occasionally as the apples begin to release their juices. Simmer for approximately 10 minutes. Apples should be cooked, but not mushy.

To prepare the pancakes: Mix flours, baking powder, baking soda, and salt in bowl. In separate bowl, beat together the buttermilk, eggs, milk, honey, and oil. Stir the wet ingredients into the dry ingredients, only enough to blend, do not overmix. Gently stir in the hemp seeds. Cook batter in desired-size pancakes on a hot griddle or in a hot pan.

Serve with warm apple compote, dried cranberries, and real maple syrup.

TED'S BULLETIN

505 8TH STREET SE
WASHINGTON, DC 20003
(202) 544-8337
TEDSBULLETIN.COM
EXECUTIVE CHEF/OWNER: ERIC BRANNON

If sprinkles on Pop Tarts and meat loaf with ketchup get you humming about a few of your favorite things, then you should get your gravy-loving soul to Ted's Bulletin as soon as possible. The Barrack's Row diner-style restaurant offers a menu of old-school American dishes against the backdrop of a 1930s-style decor. The Shake-N-Bake Fried Chicken stands out as a favorite among this menu of favorites. Added bonus: It even comes wrapped in paper minus the string.

I definitely grew up eating Shake 'n Bake and I loved that herby flavor it would always have," says Chef Eric Brannon who came up with this retro dish served at Ted's Bulletin, a twist on the old suppertime standby. "When we came up with our menu we thought about the things we loved eating growing up . . . this was one of them."

Brannon's recipe also contains a pickle brine shout out to a fast food chicken he liked. When he discovered that back in the day the readymade chicken he enjoyed was pickle-brined before it was fried, he decided to do the same with the fried chicken he created for Ted's. The brining adds a hint of flavor and also helps tenderize the meat. For those attempting the recipe at home, he encourages using a whole chicken, assuring first-timers that cleaning a whole chicken really is a lot easier than people think. (It's also a lot cheaper than buying the pieces already cut and cleaned.) If you are feeling adventurous and want to give it a try, Brannon suggests doing a search online for video that walks you through the steps—there are many out there although none that I can find at this time done to Julie Andrews's tunes.

SHAKE-N-BAKE FRIED CHICKEN

YIELD: 2 FRIED BREASTS, WINGS, LEGS, AND THIGHS

1 whole chicken, quartered
1½ cups seasoned flour (see recipe below)
1 cup egg wash (see recipe below)
Brine (see recipe below)
1½ quarts vegetable oil for frying

For seasoned flour:

½ cup cornmeal
½ cup Italian seasoned bread crumbs
2 cups all-purpose flour
1 tablespoon Cajun spice
2 teaspoons chopped rosemary
2 teaspoons chopped thyme
2 teaspoons chopped parsley
1 teaspoon dried oregano
1 tablespoon salt
1 teaspoon black pepper

For the egg wash:

5 eggs
3 ounces water
2 tablespoons hot sauce

For the brine:

2 cups pickle juice
4 cups water
3 sprigs rosemary
2 sprigs thyme
1 tablespoon salt
1 tablespoon pepper

To prepare the seasoned flour: Mix all ingredients together until well incorporated.

To prepare the egg wash: Mix all ingredients together until well incorporated.

To prepare the brine: Mix all ingredients together until well incorporated.

To assemble: Cut chicken, place in brine, and refrigerate for 2 hours. Heat fryer or oil in a deep frying pan to 275°F.

Dredge chicken in seasoned flour, then in egg wash, then back in the seasoned flour until well coated. Place chicken in oil and fry for 12–14 minutes until golden brown and cooked all the way through. Use caution when frying and keep water away from oil. Only use a pan that has enough depth to leave half of the pan without oil.

After frying is complete, keep chicken warm in oven or let rest for 4 minutes before serving. Enjoy with your favorite dipping sauces.

Vidalia

1990 M Street NW
Washington, DC 20036
(202) 659-1990
VIDALIADC.COM
Chef/Co-Owner: Jeffrey Buben
Co-Owner: Sallie Buben; Chef de Cuisine: Hamilton Johnson

It seems only natural that a restaurant named for a variety of onion would feature said onion on its menu. But shining a spotlight on the restaurant's namesake was not part of the original plan at Vidalia.

"The baked Vidalia onion was Sallie's idea," tells Chef Jeffrey Buben, who co-owns the Southern-focused restaurant with his wife, Sallie. "We at the restaurant balked at it at first, thinking who is going to come in looking for a baked onion? The first night at Vidalia everyone asked where the baked onion was on the menu. The very next day we formulated the prototype for Vidalia's baked onion and it's been a staple ever since."

Rather than just rest on the success of that first onion dish, Buben made the decision to add a new one every year. "We did not want to be complacent so we have a contest each year for the staff to come with new variations of the baked onion."

Vidalia's Baked Onion with Spring Garlic Shoots, Mushrooms & Red-Eye Gravy is a recent winner and combines many of the tastes that have kept Vidalia a DC favorite since it first opened its doors back in 1993. When you make the winning recipe at home, remember to let the onions sit in their own liquid after removing them from the oven, which allows them to retain their juices and flavors. The onion-savvy chefs at Vidalia also advise leaving a bit of the root intact so that the onion stays together. It also makes for a prettier final presentation.

Baked Onion with Spring Garlic Shoots, Mushrooms & Red-Eye Gravy

SERVES 8

4 jumbo Vidalia onions

¼ cup extra-virgin olive oil

2 cups king trumpet or shiitake mushrooms, washed and sliced

1 cup spring garlic shoots (or leeks), washed and chopped

2 slices country ham, julienned

¼ cup sherry vinegar

1½ cups beef broth or bouillon

½ cup strong black coffee

¼ cup light brown sugar

½ cup tomato, peeled, seeded and chopped

2 teaspoons fresh thyme, chopped

2 teaspoons fresh rosemary, chopped

Salt and freshly ground pepper to taste

4 teaspoons chives, minced

Preheat oven to 375°F. Peel the onions and remove core. Trim the bottom of the onion as close to the base of the onion as possible without causing the petals to separate. This will allow it to lay flat, but stay intact.

Heat the extra-virgin olive oil in a large saucepan or oven roaster pan over medium-high heat and place the onions in the pan, core side down. Add the mushrooms, spring garlic shoots, and country ham. Stir until they begin to brown slightly—this should take about 2–3 minutes. Add the vinegar, beef broth, coffee, and brown sugar. Stir into mixture until the sugar dissolves. Add the tomato, thyme, and rosemary. Season mixture with salt and pepper to taste. Cover the pan with aluminum foil.

Place the covered pan in the oven. Baste the onions with the pan liquid periodically until they are tender—about 45 minutes to 1 hour.

Remove the pan from the oven and let rest for 10 minutes. Transfer the onions to a serving plate. Place the pan with liquid back on medium-high heat and reduce slightly until a light glaze occurs, about 2–3 minutes. Adjust seasoning to taste and spoon the mixture over the onions.

Sprinkle with minced chives and serve.

VOLT

228 NORTH MARKET STREET
FREDERICK, MARYLAND 21701
(301) 696-8658
VOLTRESTAURANT.COM
EXECUTIVE CHEF/CO-OWNER: BRYAN VOLTAGGIO

The popular reality show *Top Chef* put Bryan Voltaggio's face on TV, but it was his ability to take farm-to-table dining off script that placed him at the top of the restaurant scene before the cameras ever switched on. After climbing the ranks of prestigious Manhattan kitchens, Bryan moved back to his hometown of Frederick, Maryland, to open Volt in 2008. The phone lines have been buzzing ever since.

One of those early calls came from the *Top Chef* producers, inviting him to compete on the show after realizing they had hit reality show gold: brothers who are both chefs. "They basically called me up and asked me do you want to come on the show and kick your brother's ass," he says with a slight smirk as he bends down and picks fallen leaves out from the raised beds in the garden beside Volt. In the end, Bryan came in second to his brother, Chef Michael Voltaggio, but he is quick to say he looks back at it as a fun and worthwhile experience. That was back in 2009 and diners and critics still can't get enough of the restaurant from the chef with inked-up arms and laser-beam focus. Volt still ranks as an "it" reservation for Washingtonians despite the forty-five-minute drive up north to get there, and a coveted spot at Table 21, the Chef's Table, still is considered serious foodie street cred.

Although his other ventures (two in Frederick and one in Chevy Chase to date) and commitments (be it hanging with the first lady at the White House Easter-egg roll or promoting his cookbook on *Late Night with Jimmy Fallon*) take him away from Volt, his staff knows the kitchen is the prize on days he is in the house. Come three in the afternoon on most days when he's at Volt, Voltaggio and his intense focus are in the kitchen of the restaurant he opened in the town where he grew up. Turns out you can go home again.

CRAB SUMMER ROLL

SERVES 4

For crabmeat:

1 teaspoon grape-seed oil
½ shallot, minced
1 cup crabmeat
1 tablespoon spicy aioli (recipe below)
⅛ teaspoon salt
1 cilantro sprig, picked leaves only

For yuzu vinaigrette:

3 ounces yuzu juice
3½ ounces orange juice
1½ ounces fresh ginger, peeled and chopped
2 stalks lemongrass, chopped
1 teaspoon sugar
¼ bunch cilantro
¼ teaspoon Dijon mustard
2 cups blended vegetable oil

For aioli:

3 whole large eggs
4 large egg yolks
2 tablespoons chili powder
½ teaspoon sriracha
1 tablespoon mae ploy
1 tablespoon plus 2 teaspoons salt
1¾ cup grape-seed oil

For soy air:

10 tablespoons plus 1 teaspoon water
5 tablespoons soy sauce
½ teaspoon soy lecithin
1 tablespoon mirin

For avocado wrap:

3 avocados
1 teaspoon grape-seed oil

To assemble:

Rice paper
Micro cilantro

To prepare the crabmeat: Put the grape-seed oil in a small sauté pan set over medium heat. Once the oil begins to shimmer, add the shallot and cook 3–5 minutes until tender but not browned. Let the shallot cool to room temperature. Put the crabmeat in a mixing bowl, gently picking through it to remove any stray bits of shell or cartilage. Add the shallots, aioli, salt, and cilantro. Gently mix everything together. Store in a lidded container in the refrigerator for up to 2 days.

To prepare the yuzu vinaigrette: Put the yuzu juice, orange juice, ginger, lemongrass, and sugar into a saucepot set over medium heat and bring to a simmer. Cook until the liquid is reduced by half—about 10 minutes. Remove from the heat, add the cilantro and let cool to room temperature—about 20 minutes. Strain the liquid and transfer it to a small mixing bowl. Add the Dijon mustard and whisk them together. Once fully incorporated, slowly whisk in the oil until it has all been emulsified into the mustard mixture. Reserve.

To prepare the aioli: In a blender combine the 3 whole eggs, egg yolks, chili powder, sriracha, mae ploy, and salt. Turn the blender on low speed and slowly increase to a medium speed. Drizzle in the oil in a slow, steady stream until emulsified. Use immediately or transfer to a lidded container and store in the refrigerator for up to three days.

To prepare the soy air: Put the water, soy sauce, soy lecithin, and mirin in a tall, narrow container. Blend with an immersion blender to form a light, airy foam.

To make the avocado wrap: Peel Avocados but leave them whole. Using a peeler, peel the avocado flesh in long thin strips. Line on a piece of square parchment that has been seasoned with oil to help release.

To finish: Lay one sheet of rice paper that has been soaked and is ready to be worked on a cutting board. On one side, lay ¼ inch of mixed crab on top and shape it to cover the width of the paper at 3½ inches. Roll the paper with crab inside to resemble a sushi roll. Cut into three even pieces. Place the avocado strips on the plate in a snake-like shape onto a plate. Place the three pieces of crab roll around the avocado, one on each end and one near the middle of the avocado. Pour yuzu vinaigrette into a squeeze bottle to put six dots on the plate around the components. Garnish with micro cilantro, buzz the soy air with an immersion blender to refresh. Scoop foam off the top with a spoon and place two large spoonfuls on top of the two crab rolls.

Whisked!

(202) 656-4890
WHISKEDDC.COM
@WHISKEDDC
Owner/Baker: Jenna Huntsberger

Jenna Huntsberger did the baker's equivalent of running away and joining the circus. After coming to DC from Oregon to work for political advocacy groups, the pull of butter artfully mixed with sugar got the best of her and she left the world of 9-to-5 (it's DC so make that 9-to-9) for the world of oven timers and parchment paper. Huntsberger left the allure of political organizations to break into the world of food. She started her Modern Domestic blog and took on a series of part-time jobs that required her to spend her days in or near kitchens. Among them were stints at SouperGirl and The Big Cheese food truck before going out on her own to start her pie-focused business, Whisked!.

Her time at Soupergirl and The Big Cheese each helped carve out the path that led to Whisked! Like Soupergirl, Huntsberger operates on a subscription basis where customers pre-order pies—savory and sweet—and then pick them up at predetermined locations. (She also sells her baked goods at the Bloomingdale Farmers' Market.) The

service recently morphed into the area's first pie CSA. Huntsberger scours the markets for the freshest ingredients of the moment, bakes them into her perfectly constructed pie crusts, and then offers them to her subscribers. It's her way of baking what is best and local into her business.

While Soupergirl serves as something of the business model and mentor, it's The Big Cheese that sparked the idea for the Nutella Banana Pie, her most popular dessert. The truck offered a Nutella banana desert sandwich, and while she was making them in the mobile kitchen one day it occurred to her that the combination would also make a great pie filling.

"I made it a bazillion times," she recalls. "So I asked my boss if I could steal his flavor combo and make it into a pie."

Nutella Banana Pie

MAKES 1 9-INCH PIE

For the crust:

½ cup plus 2 tablespoons (3 ounces)
  graham cracker crumbs
1 tablespoon plus 1½ teaspoons (¾ ounce)
  dark brown sugar
Pinch of salt
2½ tablespoons (1¼ ounces) butter, melted

For the Nutella layer:

1 ounce semisweet chocolate
4 ounces Nutella

For the banana pudding:

1 large, very ripe banana (4 ounces), sliced lengthwise
1 tablespoon sugar (for sprinkling on bananas)
¹⁄₃ cup plus 1½ teaspoons (2½ ounces) sugar
  (for the pudding)
2 tablespoons (½ ounce) cornstarch
¹⁄₈ teaspoon salt
2 egg yolks
1 cup whole milk
¼ cup evaporated milk
2 tablespoons (1 ounce) butter
½ teaspoon vanilla extract

For the garnish:

¼ cup hazelnuts, lightly toasted and roughly chopped

To prepare the crust: Preheat the oven to 350°F. In a large bowl, mix together the graham cracker crumbs, dark brown sugar, and salt until evenly combined. Pour in the melted butter and mix into the dry mixture—crumbs should be damp and clump together if you pinch them with your fingers.

Carefully pat the crust mixture into the sides and bottom of a pie tin.

Bake for 10 minutes, until the crust is lightly toasted. Let cool.

To prepare the Nutella layer: In a small bowl microwave the chocolate on a low-power setting in 10 second intervals until melted, stirring occasionally. Stir into the Nutella until combined. Reserve 2 tablespoons of the mixture for garnishing the tart and carefully spread the remaining Nutella mixture in an even layer on the bottom of the crust (the easiest way to do this is to gently spread the filling with lightly wet fingers).

To prepare the banana pudding: Place the bananas in a shallow baking pan and sprinkle with the 1 tablespoon of sugar. Roast for 20–25 minutes until bananas are soft and sugar is caramelized. Transfer to a food processor and process until smooth.

In a saucepan, combine the ⅓ cup plus 1½ teaspoons of sugar, cornstarch, and salt. Whisk in the yolks. Gradually pour in the whole milk and evaporated milk, whisking until combined.

Heat mixture over moderate heat and bring to a simmer. Stir continuously as the mixture thickens. Let simmer for 1 minute, until the mixture is shiny and the cornstarch is cooked through. Take off the heat and mix in butter and vanilla extract.

Pour the mixture into the food processor and process with the banana until smooth. Strain and pour into the graham cracker crust, over the Nutella layer. Smooth top with a small offset spatula. Place plastic wrap directly on the surface of the pudding topping and refrigerate until set, about 2 hours.

To assemble: When set, drizzle or pipe the remaining Nutella mixture over the top of pie decoratively and garnish with chopped hazelnuts. Serve chilled.

Brownie Sandwich Cookies

MAKES 26 HALVES, 13 COOKIES

2 cups all-purpose flour
½ cup (1½ ounces) cocoa powder, sifted
2 teaspoons baking powder
½ teaspoon salt
16 ounces semisweet chocolate chips, melted
4 eggs
2 teaspoons vanilla extract
2 teaspoons espresso powder
10 tablespoons (5 ounces) butter, softened
½ cup (3½ ounces) granulated sugar
1¼ cups (10½ ounces) dark brown sugar
Vanilla cream (see page 195)

Special equipment: A number 20 scoop

Preheat the oven to 350°F. In a medium bowl, whisk together the all-purpose flour, cocoa (sift the cocoa if it is lumpy), baking powder, and salt.

Place semisweet chocolate chips in a small bowl and microwave on low power, for 20 seconds. Remove from microwave and stir, then microwave for another 20 seconds on low power. Repeat melting and stirring process until chocolate is completely melted.

In a small bowl, gently mix the eggs and vanilla extract. Sprinkle over the espresso powder to dissolve.

In the bowl of a stand mixer fitted with a paddle attachment, cream the butter, sugar, and dark brown sugar until fluffy. Add the egg mixture and beat until combined, scraping down the sides of the bowl if needed. Beat in the melted chocolate until combined.

Gradually add the flour mixture until combined.

Let batter sit for half an hour to set before scooping with a number 20 cookie scoop. Place halves on a baking sheet lined with parchment paper, leaving at least 2 inches between cookies. Bake for 16–18 minutes, until edges are set but centers still look slightly raw. Let cool completely before filling with vanilla cream.

Vanilla Cream

YIELDS ABOUT 1 QUART

8 ounces (2 sticks) butter, softened
3 cups (12 ounces) powdered sugar
1 teaspoon vanilla extract
¼ teaspoon kosher salt

In the bowl of a stand-up mixer fitted with a paddle attachment, beat the butter until creamy. Add the powdered sugar and beat until light and fluffy—about 5 minutes. Beat in vanilla extract and kosher salt until combined.

ZAYTINYA

701 9TH STREET NW
WASHINGTON, DC 20001
(202) 638-0800
ZAYTINYA.COM
CHEF/OWNER: JOSÉ ANDRÉS
HEAD CHEF: MICHAEL COSTA

At first glance it could have been a scene playing out in almost any living room in almost any town, anywhere in America. A then nine-year-old Michael Costa was glued to his family's TV, completely absorbed in the program before him. But when you zoomed in on the action, it wasn't a sitcom or a tied game that was drawing him in. Instead it was a chef preparing a chocolate soufflé that had so completely and fully captured his attention.

"I was watching an episode of *The Great Chefs of San Francisco* and decided I wanted to make a soufflé," tells Costa, who grew up in Woodbridge, Virginia, and always remembers being interested in cooking. "So my mom and I went to the library and took out a book on soufflés and we made one."

The soufflé, Costa reports all these years later, did not fall, although he is quick to add they might have overcooked it a bit. Any eye for perfection and detail in the kitchen that no doubt still serves him well as the head chef of the always-busy Mediterranean small-plates José Andrés's restaurant, Zaytinya.

The simple yet striking Penn Quarter restaurant evokes the beauty of the Greek islands with its modern, airy feel and sea blue and pure white decor, while the menu takes its inspiration from Turkish, Greek, and Lebanese flavors. These two dishes serve as great examples of how the restaurant combines those food traditions while keeping them current. At Zaytinya Costa uses a feta imported from Greece for the Htipiti, which is less salty and softer than the ones sold here. A heavier emphasis on salting stands as one of the keys to the brussels sprouts dish, Costa shares. The salt cuts the bitterness of the brussels sprouts, thereby allowing diners to truly enjoy the flavor of the vegetable that sometimes gets a bad rap. Clearly it works. The Brussels Sprouts Afelia holds the title as the most requested recipe at the Zaytinya.

Htipiti

SERVES 2

4 red bell peppers
1 clove garlic
1 shallot, peeled
3 tablespoons red wine vinegar
¼ cup extra-virgin olive oil
Dash white pepper
½ tablespoon salt
1½ tablespoons fresh thyme, stems removed
8 ounces block feta cheese

Preheat oven to 450°F degrees. Place red peppers directly on oven racks. Bake for approximately 30 minutes, turning every 7 minutes or so. When the peppers are charred, remove from the oven carefully with tongs. Set the peppers aside and let the peppers cool. Mince garlic and shallots and place in a small mixing bowl. Combine oil, vinegar, garlic, shallots, white pepper, and salt. Set aside.

Peel the charred skin from the outside of the peppers. Discard the peels, stems, and seeds. Chop the peppers into small pieces and place in medium sized mixing bowl. Whisk dressing to combine and pour over peppers. Sprinkle fresh thyme on top of pepper mixture. Coarsely chop feta into small pieces and add to pepper mixture. Stir ingredients together and chill for 15 minutes before serving.

Brussels Sprouts Afelia

SERVES 4

For the coriander ladolemono:

3 tablespoons whole coriander seeds

2 tablespoons Greek yogurt

2 tablespoons freshly squeezed lemon juice

½ cup extra-virgin olive oil

For the roasted garlic yogurt:

2 cloves roasted garlic

6 tablespoons of Greek yogurt

Sea salt to taste

¼ cup cranberries

½ cup port or other sweet wine

Olive oil for frying

1 pound brussels sprouts

Sea salt to taste

¼ cup chopped dill

2 tablespoons roasted garlic yogurt per serving

¼ cup coriander ladolemono per serving

To prepare the coriander ladolemono: Using a rolling pin, grind the coriander seeds until coarsely ground. Do not grind the seeds too finely. Whisk the coriander seeds into the Greek yogurt. Slowly add the lemon juice and olive oil and continue whisking until it forms a smooth, creamy dressing.

To prepare the roasted garlic yogurt: Using the back of a knife, mash the roasted garlic cloves. Mix into the yogurt and season with salt.

To assemble: In a small sauce pot, combine the cranberries and port. Heat over a medium flame until the port just begins to simmer. Remove from the heat and allow the cranberries to soak for 30 minutes. Remove the cranberries and reserve for the end of the recipe.

Preheat a heavy bottomed pot or deep fryer to 350°F.

Trim the ends of the brussels sprouts and discard. Remove any discolored leaves and cut into quarters.

Deep fry the brussels sprouts for about 2 minutes until golden. Do not overcook as the brussels sprouts will turn dark and become bitter. Remove from heat and drain.

Remove any excess oil with a paper towel. Toss brussels sprouts lightly with salt and chopped dill. Adjust salt to taste as needed.

To plate: On a serving plate, spread the roasted garlic yogurt on the bottom of the plate. Arrange the brussels sprouts on top of the yogurt. Top with coriander ladolemono dressing.

Garnish with rehydrated cranberries.

ZENGO

781 7TH STREET NW
WASHINGTON, DC 20001
(202) 393-2929
RICHARDSANDOVAL.COM/ZENGODC
CHEF/OWNER: RICHARD SANDOVAL
CHEF DE CUISINE: GRAHAM BARTLETT

Chef Graham Bartlett rang in 2011 with a new scallop ceviche, a pretty version of the popular seafood appetizer that brought together avocados, crushed peanuts, cilantro, and crispy shallots. The seafood appetizer was intended to be a temporary addition to the menu at the Chinatown restaurant that artfully marries Latin and Asian flavors. Public opinion changed that.

"When I made it for [Chef Richard Sandoval], he went crazy for it," Bartlett tells of the first time he served the dish to Zengo's Chef/Owner. "He was like, just put that on the menu right now."

Long before he teamed up with Richard Sandoval, Bartlett started seriously thinking about a career in food as an undergraduate student. "I was studying English and foreign language," he tells. "I loved it. I was also working at the same time in restaurants and found I really loved going to work every day."

Following graduation, he moved to Paris and trained and worked in the restaurant world, a path that took him to several

kitchens along the way before landing him at the Washington, DC, Zengo, where he maintains and furthers Sandoval's vision and concept. But as with so many other chefs, Bartlett's personal journey with food began long before his professional one. "Food is definitely in my family," he tells, recalling dishes and meals prepared by his grandparents and others. Even his boyhood mischief can be linked to the culinary arts. When he was about five years old he got hold of his father's camera and put it in the oven. "It was a new cooking procedure," he laughs. "Roast camera."

SEA OF CORTEZ BAY SCALLOP CEVICHE WITH AVOCADO, CRUSHED PEANUTS, CILANTRO & CRISPY SHALLOTS

SERVES 4

For scallops:

Pickling spices

Pinch of salt and pepper

1 orange, quartered

1 lemon, quartered

1 pound Baja bay scallops (or if using large "dry pack" scallops, sliced)

For the ceviche liquid:

¾ cup freshly squeezed orange juice

1½ cups freshly squeezed lime juice

9 ounces Lingham's brand Malaysian chili sauce

1½ cups sweet chili sauce (recipe below)

½ cup fish sauce

For sweet chili sauce:

1 cup sugar

2 cups white vinegar

½ cup rice vinegar

1 red bell pepper, chopped in food processor

1 tablespoon minced garlic

To assemble and garnish ceviche:

2 avocados, peeled and diced

Cilantro, chopped

Peanuts, chopped

Fried shallots (available in a jar at Asian markets if you don't want to make them!)

Wonton and/or tortilla chips

To prepare the scallops: Prepare to poach the scallops, by adding the pickling spices, salt, and

pepper to a small saucepan with water. Add the orange and lemon and let simmer for about 10 minutes to flavor the poaching liquid.

Have a bowl of ice ready, then plunge scallops in boiling water for about 5 seconds. Strain and shock in ice water. They should still be slightly raw in the middle. Allow to cool completely before removing. Reserve.

To prepare the ceviche liquid: Place all ceviche ingredients in a bowl and stir them together until mixed.

To prepare the chili sauce: Cook all ingredients except garlic in a small saucepan over low heat, reducing slowly until starting to thicken. When the sauce begins to become viscous, remove from heat and stir in garlic. Cool.

To assemble the ceviche: Toss the scallops and ceviche liquid together with the avocados. Arrange in a glass bowl and garnish with the cilantro, peanuts, and shallots. Serve with chips. Makes a great appetizer for passed hors d'oeuvres served in spoons.

Recipe Index

About the Autohor & Photographer

Beth Kanter's books and articles help visitors and locals alike experience the tastes, sights, and unique feel of the nation's capital. The *Washington, DC Chef's Table* is Beth's third book about her favorite city. The author of *Food Lovers' Guide to Washington DC* and *Day Trips from Washington DC* (both Globe Pequot Press), Beth's essays and articles have appeared in national newspapers, magazines, and online. Beth has an MSJ from Northwestern's Medill School of Journalism and, when not writing about her favorite hometown, teaches writing workshops. You can visit her at bethkanter.com.

Emily Pearl Goodstein is a photographer, sweatpants enthusiast, online organizer, and rabble-rouser from Washington, DC. She leverages her status as a native Washingtonian (and expert Googler) to recommend products, restaurants, recipes, and shops (in addition to other things she finds mildly diverting) on her blog, *Wild and Crazy Pearl*. She spends too much money on iTunes and her favorite possession is the cobalt blue KitchenAid mixer that she used part of her Bat Mitzvah money to buy (it is still going strong). She also enjoys drinking grapefruit juice, photographing babies and baby bellies, and taking naps.

Photo by Tosha Francis